Things I
Wish
I'd
Known

For my boys Fraser, Caleb and Jackson,
the inspiration behind this book and everything I do,
and to Matt for believing in me.

Things I Wish I'd Known

EMILY NORRIS

Vermilion
LONDON

Vermilion, an imprint of Ebury Publishing
20 Vauxhall Bridge Road
London SW1V 2SA

Vermilion is part of the Penguin Random House group of companies
whose addresses can be found at global.penguinrandomhouse.com

Penguin
Random House
UK

Illustrations by Anya Kuvarzina 2024
Text design and chapter opener illustrations by Emily Voller

Emily Norris has asserted her right to be identified as the author of this
Work in accordance with the Copyright, Designs and Patents Act 1988

First published by Vermilion in 2024

www.penguin.co.uk

A CIP catalogue record for this book is available from the British Library

ISBN 9781785044724

Typeset in 10/15pt Qanelas by Jouve (UK), Milton Keynes
Printed and bound in Great Britain by Clays Ltd, Elcograf S.p.A.

The authorised representative in the EEA is Penguin Random House Ireland,
Morrison Chambers, 32 Nassau Street, Dublin D02 YH68

Contents

I: Home Sweet Home

Hacks

Habits

II: Food, Glorious Food

Hacks

Habits

III: Travel & Holidays

Hacks

Habits

IV: School Rules

Hacks

Habits

V: Everything I've Learned About . . .

Introduction

Hello! I'm Emily, a YouTuber and busy mum to three boys. At the time of writing, Fraser, Caleb and Jackson are thirteen, ten and seven and we've also got a cavapoo called Kiki, so you can probably imagine, it's pretty crazy in our house. But I wouldn't change it for the world.

First of all, I want to thank you for picking up my book. I chose the title *Things I Wish I'd Known* because it is crammed full of exactly that – all the things, big and small, I wish I'd known before embarking on each ever-changing stage of motherhood.

Every single hack and habit I've written about here has been tried and tested on my own family and I hope you find plenty of useful ideas and pointers to help make your everyday a little easier.

Let me explain what I mean by 'hacks' and 'habits' and how they are going to take shape over the coming pages:

Hack: a quick, clever (and often fun) solution to a parenting problem and something you can implement right away. Bingo!

Habit: a longer-term, behavioural and routine-based remedy focused on running your household as efficiently as possible. Habits require a bit more thought and planning, but don't worry, I'm here to help you with all of that.

Being a parent is hard. It can be boring and lonely and stressful and it's OK to say that out loud – those are feelings we all experience and they are totally valid. But I truly believe that even the mundane side of motherhood can actually be rather lovely and I always try to celebrate and elevate that. There is joy to be found even in the humdrum.

Which brings me to why I do what I do and, I guess, the reason this book exists. I've not spoken about this before, but I feel like it's the right time to open up a bit more about my own childhood, which was extremely chaotic and filled with a lot of sadness and upheaval.

My dad was a violent alcoholic with all sorts of addiction issues and we lived in constant fear of him. Eventually, my mum took me and my sister away to live with my grandparents where we found a safe haven for a while. But then she met my stepdad who was ex-Navy and an authoritarian with a quick temper and again I found myself in a house where I didn't feel safe.

We were scared of him. When he came home from work, we could tell what mood he'd be in by the way he closed the door – if it was with a slam, we'd know to hide. My mum had my sister at 18 and me at 20, so she was very young and life could be tough. I'd go to friends' houses where family life was so settled and 'normal' and I remember desperately wanting that for myself.

And that's where my love of home comforts comes from. It's why I take such pleasure in creating a peaceful, happy, regular household – I want to give my boys the stable and carefree childhood I always craved.

Although both my dad and stepdad have since died, the memories of living with their abuse are still vivid and raw and that is what drives me. I used to imagine having a family of my own one day, where we had roots and security and baked banana bread. A place where no one ever felt scared. I have that now and I will never not appreciate it.

That said, my motherhood journey hasn't always been plain-sailing. I started sharing parenting videos and my experience of being a mum on YouTube back in 2014, when I was feeling a bit isolated at home on maternity leave with a baby and a pre-schooler. I'd gone from being a busy marketing director to just 'mummy', and when my husband Matt returned home from working long hours at the end of each day, I felt a bit silly only having stories of dirty nappies and (a lack of) sleep to regale him with!

I loved being a full-time mum to my boys, but I missed the adult interaction I'd had at work and, as a result, my self-confidence took a knock. I live in England, but all my family are in Canada and I missed them more than ever – it's weird because although I barely had a second on my own, in many ways I'd never felt more alone.

One thing I really enjoyed from spending time on YouTube was getting tips and ideas from other mums. Picking up simple tricks (or 'hacks') while juggling the ups and downs of mother-hood saved me precious time, energy and money – they even saved my sanity on more than one occasion!

The first time I ever heard of a 'mum hack' was when a friend taught me that baby vests were designed with an envelope neck, so that in the event of an explosive poo, you could easily pull the vest down over the body to remove it, rather than lifting it over their head, causing carnage in the process. My mind was blown. I'd had two babies by that point and couldn't believe I was only just learning this now!

Over the next few hundred pages, you will find my most popular hacks as well as plenty of new ones I've been saving, making this book (I hope!) your ultimate go-to resource for all things parenting. It's super simple to use:

- Each of the first four sections – Home Sweet Home, Food, Glorious Food, Travel & Holidays, School Rules – is split into two parts: one for hacks and another for habits.

- In the fifth and final section, Everything I've Learned About, we'll look at some of the 'bigger picture' issues around parenting that I often talk about on my channel such as sleep, boundary pushing and post-baby relationships with partners and I'll be sharing what worked – and continues to work – for us as a family while navigating these notorious minefields.

- You don't have to read the book in order, just turn to the area you want at any given time and refer back as and when you need.

- Most of the hacks and habits don't require any special equipment, however, some chapters include a short list of items you may not necessarily have as standard in the house, but which might come in handy.

- You will find child-related hacks and habits that are applicable to newborns all the way up to teenagers and, where appropriate, I have suggested adjustments depending on the age of your children.

- Watch out for the 'Game-Changing Gadgets' which pop up now and again – these are inexpensive, time-saving products which I love because they do a job and do it well.

4

- I've included some of our favourite family breakfast, lunch and dinner recipes and ideas in Chapter 12. These are all fail-safes in our house; they're super simple to make and many are brilliant for batch cooking, which I swear by.

- And because I don't know a single mum who takes enough time for herself, sprinkled throughout the pages you'll find my 'Moment For You' ideas, which I hope will encourage you to press pause on everything else and prioritise yourself for a little while.

Before we get going, I want to let you know that if you're feeling overwhelmed and thinking you'll never get on top of it all because the house is too cluttered and life is too chaotic, I'm not a naturally organised person either. Being tidy and structured is something I have to work at and I need strategies to help me stay on track. I guess it's a bit like going to the gym. Not many of us particularly enjoy getting there but if we like the results, it's worth sticking at.

So please don't feel that you're forever destined to live your life like it's a precariously balanced house of cards. This book is here for you and this is the beginning.

Finding a hack to make things feel a little bit more manageable can give you a lift. Find three or four and you're seriously winning! So let's see what we can achieve together and how a few clever tricks and tweaks can completely transform family life. Maybe it'll be a great routine that leads to more co-operative children in the morning, a cleaning hack that makes your home sparkling clean in a fraction of the time, a laundry tip that saves you money or a tweak to the night-time schedule which transforms everyone's sleep.

Shall we do it? Let's get started!

I.

Home
Sweet
Home

Someone once told me that running a household is like running a business and I do think there's some truth in that. So many of us are managing careers, multiple school runs, childcare arrangements and keeping a home on top of trying to be a good parent who spends quality time with their children. And that multitude of demands can feel completely overwhelming. Gosh, I hear you!

Finding easy ways to keep all the plates spinning at home is key to relieving some of those pressures and I've discovered some brilliant hacks over the years to help with that.

Sure, the odd plate will drop now and again (OK, sometimes several at once!) but if you can feel like you're on top of things *most* of the time then, believe me, you're nailing it.

In this section I'll be sharing tips on keeping the children entertained on rainy days without destroying the house, how to clean, tidy and get through the bottomless laundry pile while making the process quicker and more enjoyable (yes, really!), how to ensure that everyone chips in and does their fair share so that the load doesn't fall on one over-worked person, as well as plenty of clever hacks to solve everyday household headaches.

Hacks

Chapter 1

Rainy Day Remedies

Living in the UK means you can never truly rely on the weather to play ball, so over the years I've gathered a whole repertoire of activities for the days when we're stuck in the house. I've split them into three categories – crafts, games and educational – so you can easily pick and choose. You'll find ideas to suit kids of all ages that will keep them occupied and stop us parents going stir crazy. Enjoy!

YOU MAY NEED:

- Freezer bags
- Paint sample cards
- Balloons
- Painters' tape
- Toothpicks
- Marshmallows
- Alka-Seltzer tablets
- Hard-coated, colourful fruit sweets

CRAFTS

Mess-Free Painting

Whenever I've shared this one on my YouTube channel or Instagram, it's been a huge hit and the feedback is always incredible. So I reckon it's the perfect hack to kick this book off with! Take a freezer bag and put a few different coloured blobs of paint inside. Seal it up, tape it to a window and let your children move the paint around with their fingers – because the paint is sealed inside, they won't get messy. And neither will your sofa/carpets/walls ... When the colours mix together and the light comes through the window, it almost has a stained-glass effect and toddlers especially love this.

Sparkly Pasta Jewellery

Use penne pasta and decorate with felt tips or add a bit of glue and roll the shapes in some glitter. Thread a length of string through the holes and make necklaces or bracelets. This is also great for building up fine motor skills for little ones. As an alternative to pasta, you can cut up paper straws into 2cm pieces.

Colourful Ice Paints

A quick confession: this is fairly messy so it might not be for everyone! Ice painting is an activity you can have in your freezer, all ready for whenever you need it. Fill some ice-cube trays with each compartment two-thirds full of water and one third of paint (food colouring will work as an alternative). Place in the freezer with lolly sticks or toothpicks in them as a handle and let the cubes freeze. Once frozen, you can remove each one from the tray and hold the sticks, using them like paintbrushes. Paint on to a sheet of white cardboard – you can use the reverse side of old Christmas and birthday cards here. As the cubes melt, they'll make creative swirly designs on the card.

Best Playdough Ever

My favourite playdough recipe, which I've been making for years, only has two ingredients and neither is what you'd expect: cornflour and hair conditioner. I swear this works using two parts cornflour to one part hair conditioner which I pick up from budget shops. The conditioner means the playdough smells lovely and I always find that I have really soft hands after we've played with it. You can add food colouring, which is best added to the conditioner before you mix it with the cornflour. Store in an airtight container to keep it fresh for another day.

DIY Slime

Kids can't get enough slime, can they? You can make your own at home by using roughly equal amounts of cornflour and washing-up liquid. You may not thank me for this one though as it's very, well, slimy!

Make Your Own Paint

Before you throw away dried-out felt tip pens, soak them in a small jar of water. Let them sit overnight and the remaining ink from the pen will seep into the water, creating a watercolour paint which you can store in the lidded jar.

Easy Peely Stickers

This is one of my favourite mum hacks ever! If your child struggles to peel stickers off the sheet, remove the liner around all the stickers first – pull it off from the corner of the sheet. This makes it so much easier for little fingers to peel the individual stickers off themselves.

Allow YouTube to Parent

I know none of us want to encourage more screen time, but You-Tube tutorials can be a great resource. My children love drawing and really enjoy following the 'how to' videos step-by-step – they're always so proud of the end result. If your child loves dance, football or even yoga there are great follow-along tutorials that would be perfect for a rainy day.

Making the Cut

Little ones find it difficult to master the art of holding scissors. To help, draw a smiley face (or pop a sticker) on your child's thumbnail and tell them to keep the face upwards while cutting, which will teach them the correct way to hold and snip.

Clever Colouring In

Quick and easy one for you here – when the kids are colouring in, tape the corners of the paper to the table so it doesn't slip around. And to avoid buying whole colouring books that may only get a few uses because the kids aren't interested in every picture on every page, we search 'colouring pages' online for their favourite characters and print them out at home.

GAMES

DIY Surprise Eggs

My kids love anything with an element of surprise, especially if it comes inside a chocolate egg . . . but obviously I don't always want them to have the chocolate or plastic toy. This DIY version is a fun and creative activity that you can do with playdough. Gather some small objects like toy cars and mini figures, and wrap them individually in an egg-shaped playdough ball, hide them around the house and watch the joy as they open them up and discover what's inside. We did a festive version of this at Christmas with some socks. The boys would pretend to sleep while I filled the socks with small toys I'd gathered up from around the house and when they woke up, they loved opening their pretend Christmas stockings.

Rainbow Scavenger Hunt

Next time you're at a hardware or interiors store, pick up a few paint swatch sample cards featuring as many different colours as you can. Let your children choose one of the cards and get them to find items in the house that match each of the colours on there. The first one to find an item in every colour is the winner!

Balloon Tennis

We do this with makeshift rackets which are simply wooden spoons secured with tape to the back of paper plates left over from birthday parties. Get two of these ready and then blow up a balloon which the kids can hit between them using the rackets. It's a tennis match that will keep them busy for a while and is gentle enough to ensure your living room stays in one piece.

For toddlers, as an alternative to the tennis, tie a string to a balloon and tape it hanging downwards from the ceiling, low enough for your little one to reach. They will enjoy bopping it around.

Painters' Tape Assault Course

I discovered the delights of painters' tape when we were doing a lot of decorating around the house. It's what painters and decorators use to mask off areas in order to create straight lines, but I use it to create an obstacle course! I stick lots of strips at various angles from left to right across the hallway creating an elaborate web which the kids have to climb through without touching any of the tape. And because it's painters' tape it's not going to damage your walls. You can make the course more elaborate for older children who are better able to contort their way through.

This tape also works well on a hard floor where you can tape out a racetrack to play with toy cars.

Cable Car Zipline

Build a little cable car using Lego – it doesn't need to be anything fancy or complicated, just a box for one of the mini figures to stand in with a gap at the top for the cable to run through. Attach it to the washing line in the garden and you can let your cable car go down the zipline, which is so much fun. It also teaches children about how the line needs to be positioned for it to work and could spark off a discussion about gravity. If the rain outside is really lashing down, or you don't have a garden, you can adapt this game for indoors using a piece of string attached between points in the house – a tall kitchen cupboard and a doorknob would work well.

Homemade Marble Run

Save up your toilet and kitchen paper rolls and get hold of a large empty cardboard storage box. Trim down the edges so you have a tray-like structure. Position four rolls to form two lower case 'y' shapes, stacked but connected, one on top of the other, on the inside of the box tray. Cut a hole in each tube to allow the marble to drop down into the next one once it's set off down the opening at the top. Then glue or tape the rolls down in position.

For younger ones, use the painters' tape I mentioned above to make a diagonal chute with kitchen paper rolls on the wall which they can drop the marble down again and again. You could even attach two opposing marble runs to the wall and have a race!

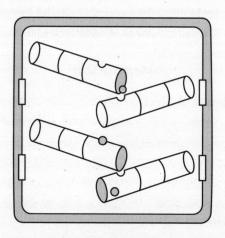

Sticky Spider Web

Get some sticky tape and secure strips of it across an open doorway, criss-crossing in lots of different angles and with the sticky side facing into the room. Then screw up coloured tissue paper into little balls (each child gets a different colour) and they can take it in turns to throw them at the sticky spider web. Whoever gets the most stuck is the winner!

Floor Is Lava

This is a firm favourite in our house and it's a game that children of all ages can get involved with. Give them an A to B route and tell them, for example, to get from the couch to the slide in the garden without touching the 'lava' (aka the floor). They'll have to get a bit creative and use different objects to step on to reach their destination, which means there are normally cushions everywhere by the end of the game! It's also a great one if you ever need to get reluctant kids into the bath. Tell them that 'the floor is lava' and the challenge is to get from the living room to the bathroom without stepping on the lava – it works (almost) every time.

Memory Test

My mother-in-law showed me this one. Collect about 10 random objects or toys from around your house, place them on a tray and ask the kids to have a good look. Cover up the objects with a tea towel or take the tray out of the room and remove one item. They must work out which object is missing. I started doing this with the boys from about two years old and it's surprising how much they can remember.

The 'I'm Bored' Jar

Whenever my boys announce 'I'm bored' I always tell them that I have lots of cleaning and tidying that they could help me with.

Funnily enough, they're not too keen on that! We have an 'I'm Bored' jar and it's something they have helped create. Take a glass jar and then write down different activities on bits of coloured paper – obviously you have to make sure they're achievable (I'm not in the business of organising trips to the moon at the drop of a hat!). These ideas could include watching a favourite movie together, playing a board game, going on a nature walk or taking a trip to the bowling alley. Then fold them all up and put them in the jar and whenever someone declares themselves 'bored', they can take a lucky dip.

EDUCATIONAL

Tin Foil Boats

Take about 30cm of tin foil and let your child scrunch and shape it into a boat shape. Float the boat in a sink filled with water or play with it at bath time. You can also add small toys or coins to see how many it can hold until it sinks. This works even better with leftover foil or takeaway containers, so save them next time you order in. Added bonus here – it might even teach your kids about physics!

Cocoa Powder Science

My boys love this cocoa powder and milk experiment. Pour some milk into a mug, then scoop up a spoonful of cocoa powder, submerge it in the milk and then bring it out again. The powder will be wet, but if you take a toothpick and poke it, it suddenly becomes completely dry again. You can do this over and over and it really is fascinating – teach the kids that this happens because cocoa powder is a hydrophobic substance, meaning that water can't enter it, so when you prick it, the layer of milk is thrown off. So cool.

Learning Pong

This game is very adaptable for all ages and to whatever subject you want them to learn about. Grab 10 plastic or paper cups and a ping pong ball. Write a series of questions down on individual pieces of paper and then pop one in every cup. For younger kids it could be colour or letter questions and for older children it might be phonics, spellings or maths questions. Let the kids bounce the ping pong ball into the cups and when it lands inside of one, you ask them the question written on the paper. Once they've answered correctly, remove that cup and repeat until all the cups are gone.

A to Z Races

Especially good for school-aged children and all you need is a timer, a pen and some paper. First write the letters of the alphabet vertically on a piece of paper and then choose a subject, such as food, animals, girls' names, boys' names, places etc. Set a timer depending on your child's age (if they're 10 and upwards try 1–2 minutes and if they're younger I'd suggest 5–6). They have to think of a word or name for each letter for the chosen category – if the category was animals, it could be Aardvark, Bear, Cat and so on. They don't have to write the answers in order and can jump around the alphabet as it's all about who has the most answers at the end of the time. (By the way, there aren't many words that start with 'X' so we bend the rules a little and say as long as the word contains an X somewhere, it counts.)

Whatever Floats Your Boat

Fill up a bowl, storage container or sink with water and then gather up small random objects or food from around the house. Ask your child what they think will sink or float. Toy cars, grapes, a tennis or golf ball, Lego pieces are all good items to try. Reward a point for every correct answer.

Pop It Quizzes

My house is full of Pop Its (silicone tray fidget toys with pokeable bubbles. If you know, you know and if you don't, you soon will!) so I was delighted to find an educational use for them. I write the alphabet or numbers on to the individual raised bits and then give the kids maths questions such as 'where are all the prime numbers?'. They need to press down the relevant answer by 'popping' the correct bubble. For little ones, you can ask them to find certain letters in the alphabet. It's a bit more creative than using traditional pen and paper and definitely holds their interest for longer.

Marshmallow Constellations

All you need for this are some mini marshmallows and toothpicks. Use an online image search to find some star constellations which the kids can recreate by joining the mallows with the toothpicks! The constellations might be a bit tricky for younger ones to follow, but they'll enjoy making their own creations and it always amazes me the quiet concentration this activity brings about.

Grow Your Own Rainbow

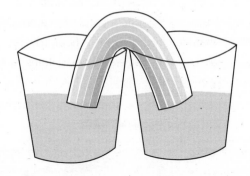

This is another cool one and all you need is two glasses of water, some felt tip pens and a paper towel. Fold your paper towel in half and trim a bit off one end so it's about 20cm long. Using felt tips, the kids should draw 5cm long rectangle blocks of rainbow colours at either end of the paper, ideally making sure both ends match. Stick each end of the paper towel into the glasses of water – as it soaks up the water, the colours start to spread, creating a rainbow which eventually meets in the middle.

DIY Lava Lamp

Take 75ml of water, some food colouring (any colour), vegetable oil and an Alka-Seltzer tablet. Fill a glass about halfway with the vegetable oil, then add the water and watch them separate. Put about 20 drops of food colouring in and then add the Alka Selt-zer tablet. The whole thing will fizz up and create a lava lamp, which will last about five mesmerising minutes.

Sweetie Rainbow

This needs to be done by an adult, but it never gets old, probably because there are sweets involved. Boil the kettle and get the kids to arrange a load of colourful fruit-flavoured, hard-coated sweets into a circle around the outside edge of a plate with all the sweets touching. Then pour the hot water into the middle of the circle and watch as the colours start to spread into the centre to form a really fabulous rainbow.

Fireworks in a Glass

Put one tablespoon of olive oil into a glass, select three or four different colours of food colouring and add 3–4 drops of each colour to the oil. Give the mixture a really good stir, which will break up the food colouring into tiny little bubbles. Then pour it into a glass of water and as the oil rises to the top, the bubbles of colouring start to separate and create little 'fireworks' that kids will love.

TV (With Strings Attached)

Sometimes needs must and a spell in front of the telly is the only answer! I saw a really funny tip on TikTok recently where the mum muted the sound on the TV and put the subtitles on, so at least the kids were reading. I guess it's a good compromise, but it made me laugh.

Stretch Out

Take a few minutes each morning to loosen up the limbs and give your muscles and joints a bit of love. Five of my favourite stretches (and the most effective) are:

CAT-COW

Get on all fours with a neutral spine. As you inhale, lift your sit bones upwards, press your chest forwards and raise your head. As you exhale, tuck the tailbone under, round the spine and release your head back down. Repeat as necessary.

COBRA

Lie flat on your tummy and place palms downwards on the floor directly under your shoulders, elbows close into the body. With your toes pointing straight backwards, inhale and gently push yourself up so your chest is raised off the floor. Hold and then come back down slowly as you exhale.

EXTENDED CHILD'S POSE

Sit on your heels, bring your feet together and set knees hip-width apart. Exhale and roll your body forward so your torso rests between your thighs. Try to keep your buttocks on your heels. Extend your arms out in front of you with your palms facing down and let your forehead gently touch the floor or mat. Breath into the stretch.

ROLLOVER

Lie flat on your back and bring your knees in together to your chest, feet off the ground. Stretch your arms out either side, palms faced down. Roll your knees over to one side and turn your head to the other. Hold for a few seconds and then come back to the middle and repeat on the opposite side.

HIP RAISES

Lie on your back with your knees bent and feet on the floor. Lay your arms out straight alongside your body, placing your palms face down and slowly raise your hips on the inhale so your bum and lower back come off the floor. On the exhale, gently come back down.

Final Word: *Sometimes a rainy day can be an opportunity to do something fun indoors and make precious memories within the four walls of home. Downpours might scupper plans, but they don't need to dampen spirits!*

Chapter 2

Cleaning & Laundry Solutions

I've never been a huge fan of cleaning although I love having a clean and tidy house so, for me, the pay-off is worth the effort. Having said that, it doesn't have to take 100 per cent effort 100 per cent of the time and there are lots of hacks I've discovered that take the sting out of everyday tasks. Some of them, dare I say it, can even become small pleasures. (OK, except for cleaning the toilet. I've yet to find a way of making that one fun!) There are hacks for every room in the house here and so without further ado, let's get our clean on . . .

YOU MAY NEED:

- White vinegar
- Rosemary sprig
- Non-stick oven liners
- Mouthwash
- Tennis balls
- Lint roller
- Magic eraser sponge
- Bicarbonate of soda
- In-wash scent beads
- Tumble dryer sheets
- Orange
- Cloves
- Empty cardboard box
- Craft knife
- Essential oils

Make Your Own All-Purpose Cleaner

Before we get down to the dirty work, I wanted to share my favourite DIY recipe for a household cleaning spray. It costs pennies to make, is eco-friendly and smells divine – tick, tick, tick! The key ingredient and the real hero of the piece is white vinegar, which is such an amazing product to have in the house and you can buy it so cheaply in bulk.

INGREDIENTS
- 250ml white vinegar
- 250ml water
- lemon rind
- rosemary sprigs

Optional: If you have essential oils, they are great for scenting. Scents are a very personal taste but lemon, eucalyptus, peppermint and lavender are a few of my favourites for cleaning.

Combine all the ingredients, pour into a spray bottle and shake thoroughly. Let the cleaner infuse for a few minutes before using. You can use the solution to clean surfaces, rubbish bins, mirrors, wall smudges and so much more. Plus, the acid from the lemon adds extra cleaning properties, which are just the job for stubborn stains.

BATHROOM

Speedy Cleaning

A refillable washing-up brush doesn't only have to be used for dirty dishes. Instead of putting washing-up liquid in the handle, fill it with an abrasive bathroom cleaner for sinks and bathtubs or a glass cleaner to clean the shower door – it's much less labour-intensive than using a cloth.

Toilet Seat Trick

Did you know that some toilet seats can be removed so you can clean them extra thoroughly? Have a look to see if yours has a button or a pinch clip at the back of the seat to release. Since I discovered this, I have not looked back – especially being a mum of boys. Say no more.

Toilet Brush Genius

If you pour a small amount of the ordinary toilet cleaner you'd use for removing limescale and tough stains into the bottom of your toilet brush holder, the brush will have some of that product on it when you come to use it. It also gets rid of any germs that are going back into the holder from the brush. This should be avoided if you have a crawling baby though.

While we're talking toilet brushes, once you've cleaned the loo, flush it to rinse off your brush and then secure the brush between the bowl and the seat. The seat will hold it in place over the bowl allowing it to air dry while you finish cleaning the rest of the bathroom. No more toilet water in the holder.

Cola Goals

Did you know that cola is The Bomb at cleaning tough limescale? For the brown limescale that forms at the bottom of the toilet bowl (often caused by hard water), first drain out the water using a mop and bucket and then fill the empty toilet with cola – full sugar not diet. Ideally leave it to soak overnight, or at least for a few hours. The carbonic and phosphoric acid in the cola helps to break down the tough stains and when you give it a scrub down afterwards, the unsightly marks should be gone.

Twinkly Taps

Cut a lemon in half and rub it over your taps and fixtures. The citric acid in the lemon helps remove hard water stains and leaves behind a fresh scent. Rinse with water and wipe dry.

Shave the Day

Shaving foam is terrific at getting out stubborn makeup stains from bathroom surfaces as well as carpets and clothes! The foam dissolves the oil and takes the mark right out.

Sparkling Shower Head

You can make your shower head shimmer and shine with a little white vinegar, which is one of my favourite multi-use products. Get a plastic bag big enough to fit over the showerhead (make sure there are no sneaky holes in the bag!) and fill it halfway with the vinegar. Place your shower head in the bag making sure it's submerged in the solution and then secure the top with some elastic bands. Leave for half an hour, remove the showerhead from the bag and give it a quick wipe with a cloth – the dirt and limescale will come off easily.

It's also worth noting that many shower heads actually screw off, which makes cleaning them so much easier. You can remove them and clean in the sink or dishwasher, unblocking any water spouts with a toothpick.

KITCHEN

Stinky Sink Fix

We all know that unmistakable smell of an unhappy sink! One tablespoon of bicarbonate of soda, a big glug of white vinegar, a capful of scented disinfectant mixed together, then run it through the plughole with hot water and it'll be as fresh as a daisy. Voila!

Micro-Wave Goodbye to Muck

How do microwaves get so gunky? And they're so awkward to clean out, but I've got a way of doing it with minimum effort. Take a medium-sized bowl, fill it about two-thirds to the top with water and add around 100ml of white vinegar.

Put the bowl in the microwave for four minutes on high, then carefully remove the bowl and wipe down the inside of the microwave with a cloth. All the congealed food should come off without a problem and you can use the warm water and vinegar solution to clean your sink afterwards for one of those 'two birds, one stone' situations we all love. If you don't have any white vinegar, water and lemon juice will do a grand job as an alternative.

Oven SOS

Ovens get dirty so quickly, but you can reduce the mess in there by using a non-stick oven liner. These can be cut to fit and they just slip inside the floor of the oven. After every few uses, take them out, wipe them down and pop them back in again.

Cleaning Blenders the Lazy Way

I like to make smoothies in the morning, but cleaning the blender afterwards was always one of my least favourite chores – until I found this hack, that is! Once you've poured out your smoothie, add some washing-up liquid and warm water to your blender, pop it back on its station and turn on the blades. The soap and water will dislodge all of the sticky bits, making it much easier to rinse off.

For the Chop

To deodorise a wooden chopping board, wet it with water and then sprinkle with bicarbonate of soda before squeezing the juice of a lemon on top – this will fizz up which is very satisfying! Leave for 10 minutes and then scrub with the remaining lemon and rinse off. It will smell divine.

Fine Fettle Kettle

Remove limescale from your kettle with our hero product white vinegar. The vinegar's acidity helps to dissolve the mineral deposits which cause the scaling. Add a mixture of equal parts water and white vinegar to your kettle and let it sit for about an hour. This allows the vinegar to break down the limescale. Then use a cleaning brush or sponge to wipe the inside of the kettle. Rinse, boil and then rinse again to get all the residue out and it'll be tip-top.

Dizzy Heights

If you're short (like me!) use a mop to clean cupboard doors that are too high up to reach easily.

Shining Example

Buff baby oil into stainless steel sinks and appliances to keep them shining and shimmering for months. Clean with a damp cloth beforehand and then use a soft cloth with a small amount of baby oil and gently wipe down. It will also remove streaks and smudges and works on silver or black stainless steel.

Dishwashers: Not Just for Dishes

I didn't realise this for years, but, once I did it was a revelation! You can use your dishwasher for anything that's waterproof, so all the plastic toys, toothbrushes, bath toys and storage containers can be bunged in and it's a great way to remove the grub and grime and sterilise at the same time.

My husband and boys love to wear caps for fashion or sport, but sweaty heads mean smelly hats so I often pop them in the dishwasher on the top rack on a normal wash with a normal tablet (although no dishes!) – I even put hairbrushes, light fittings, dust vents and extractor fan filters in there. Seriously!

No More Burnt Pans

I've managed to burn pans once or twice in my time, usually when cooking rice. But if you half-fill the pan with water, add a powdered dishwasher tablet and then gently warm it for a few minutes on the hob, the burnt pain will clean up immaculately when you wash it out.

Under the Sink Solutions

The space under the sink can often end up as one of the most cluttered areas in the house. I use extendable shelves which fit around the pipes and allow you to build a mini storage system to fit your needs. It means I can keep everything there in a semi-orderly fashion.

LAUNDRY

Chalk for Oil-Based Stains

I always thought clothes were a write-off if they were stained with any sort of grease, until I tried this. Gently rub the stain with some white chalk and then wash the item of clothing as normal and the mark will be gone.

Ditch the Iron

OK, hold on to your hats because I've got a whole list of iron-free tips, compiled over several years, dedicated to trying to avoid using one! Here we go . . .

- Put a damp cloth in the tumble dryer with the item that you want to smooth out. Just a few minutes in the dryer together will steam the item of clothing and the creases will fall out.

- Put clothes on hangers to air as soon as they're out of the machine. I pop tops and dresses straight from the washer on to a coat hanger, leave them out to dry and then put them in the wardrobe looking perfectly pressed.

- If you've forgotten about a load of laundry in the dryer and it's become all crumpled, add a couple of ice cubes to the drum and turn it back on for a few minutes. This works best when the load of washing is fairly light so there is more room for the clothes to de-crumple.

- Steam clothes in the bathroom during a hot shower.

- A crease-releasing spray will also help you dodge the iron. I always have a bottle in the house in case clothes need a quick spritz but it's really easy to make your own using 250ml of tap water, a tablespoon of white vinegar and a teaspoon of hair conditioner. You could also add in a few drops of essential oil for scent. Pour into a spray bottle and shake well to mix. Use liberally on your garment – it should be damp but not wet – and gently tug to encourage the crumples out. Hang up to dry off and the rest of the creases will simply drop out.

- I always buy the iron-free school, shirts which have got to be one of the best inventions ever!

GAME-CHANGING GADGET ALERT

- I also have a handheld steamer, which is a hassle-free alternative to the iron and have been known to use my hair straighteners to flatten out a skew-whiff shirt collar!

- Finally, turning the spin speed on your washing machine down to at least 800rpm will help reduce creases.

See, my commitment to the anti-ironing cause is strong!

Washing Machine Maintenance

If your washing machine is anything like ours and is put through its paces several times a week, it might start to get whiffy. But if you put a cup of mouthwash in the detergent section on a rinse cycle, the washer will smell amazing. The mouthwash kills the bacteria causing the odour – clever, right? It will also get rid of any mould and mildew in the process.

Anyone for Tennis?

Adding tennis balls to your dryer really speeds up the process because they stop your laundry clumping together and allow the hot air to circulate more effectively.

Direct Sunlight

I thought I couldn't love the sunshine more and then I found out its ability to bleach just about any stain out of clothing. Pasta sauce, curry and – crucially – baby poo. After washing, put the item of clothing into direct sunlight and over the course of a couple of hours it will disappear. No scrubbing required.

Pristine School Bags

It was years before it occurred to me that I might be able to wash the boys' dirty school bags in the washing machine. I thought they might end up falling apart or losing their shape, but I decided to brave it and the results were amazing! Secure any loose toggles or straps first (or pop the whole thing in a mesh bag), put it on a delicate cold cycle and it'll come out good as new and smelling fresh! How long it stays that way is another matter entirely . . .

Mark My Words!

Keep a whiteboard marker pen handy to write a reminder on the washing machine itself if there are delicate items in the wash that should not be transferred to the tumble dryer.

Fold Standard

The worst part about laundry for me is the sorting and folding afterwards, so I round up my kids to help with this and give them each a DIY cardboard clothes folding device. They're really easy to make:

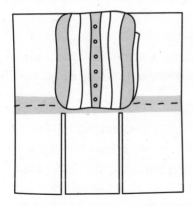 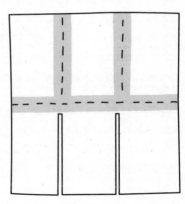

- Take an empty cardboard box and, using a craft knife, cut out six rectangular panels measuring around 20cm x 30cm.
- Lay out your panels in two rows of three, leaving a tiny gap in between each one.
- Tape each panel on the top row together and then each of them to the bottom row. Your device is now ready for folding! Place the top or shirt face down on to the middle of your board and fold the left-hand side in and back, and then

the right side. Finally, fold the bottom centre panel up then back again and you should have a perfectly folded item of clothing. The kids genuinely love doing this chore!

Chill Pills

If your gym leggings or knitwear items start pilling (you know, those pesky little balls of fluff that can form on certain fabrics?), use a razor to gently shave the bobbles off.

Heaven Scent

Make a natural deodoriser for your laundry basket, shoes or smelly football boots by using the foot of an old pair of tights or a little mesh bag and filling it with bicarbonate of soda plus around 10 drops of essential oils. The bicarb will absorb the bad odour and the essential oils will emit a new, entirely more pleasant one.

Cleaning Velcro

My boys run around on the grass at school and come home with what seems to be half the field stuck in the Velcro on their shoes. I remove this with the serrated teeth of a tape dispenser – rub the edge over the Velcro and the grass will come right out. It's oddly satisfying!

GENERAL CLEANING

Lint Roller Multitasker

A lint roller is a roll of one-sided adhesive paper attached to a central spindle with a handle and they're used for removing small fibres and hairs from clothing. But they have many more uses besides that! I use them for dusting and they're especially good for fabric bedheads and lampshades. They're also very handy for picking up small pieces of broken glass from the floor, leftover cut-offs of ribbon and paper from craft sessions and crumbs from the crevices of high chairs and carseats. I've now got a reusable lint roller that is really sticky, but you can wash and use it again and again.

Blind Spot

Take a pair of kitchen tongs, two cloths and a couple of elastic bands. Wrap a cloth around each end of the tongs (the bits you clap together) and secure in place with the bands. You've just created a tool to dust both sides of your shutter slats or blinds in one go. Spray some cleaning product on to each cloth and then use the tongs to grip and slide along each slat.

Getting the Brush Off

When I wash my hairbrushes (don't worry, I only do this every four months or so when they really need it), I pull out all the hair with tweezers or a fork and then use a little bit of shampoo, water and an old toothbrush to give them a good scrub and rinse.

For makeup brushes, mix washing-up liquid with olive oil (50/50) for a great cleaner. The olive oil loosens the makeup while the soap cleans the brush. Just leave your brushes to soak in the solution for an hour or so and then rinse off and let them air dry.

Box Fresh Trainers

This is a simple way to brighten up white trainers. Put some toothpaste on to the grubby areas, rub in using an old toothbrush and leave for a few minutes before giving them a really good scrub and wiping it off.

GAME-CHANGING GADGET ALERT

Magic Trick

Magic eraser sponges are proper miracle workers! You can pick them up really cheaply in bulk from most supermarkets and bargain stores and they're amazing for cleaning all sorts of things. They remove fingerprints, crayon and even permanent marker from walls. They can revive grotty tile grout and clean off those little coloured marks bath toys sometimes leave on the bath. You can also use them to clean shoes and trainers. Incredible.

Bicarbonate of Soda to the Rescue

We've all been there, when our child doesn't quite make it to the bathroom in time and vomits on the carpet. Not fun. Most carpet and upholstery cleaners will get rid of the stain, but the smell can linger and that's where bicarbonate of soda can come to the rescue. Clean up the area, then sprinkle a generous amount of bicarbonate of soda over the stain, leave for a few hours (or even overnight if you can) before vacuuming up.

Make Your House Smell Amazing

I like to place tumble dryer sheets throughout the house for a fresh scent which isn't overpowering. I put them among artificial flowers, in bedrooms behind scatter cushions, in drawers and inside football boots. If you'd prefer a natural alternative, try making your own perfume balls by taking an orange (or any other citrus fruit) and studding it with cloves. Hang or place them around the home and they will last up to a week, possibly longer if you store them in the fridge overnight.

Dust Your Light Bulbs

This is something I never used to think of doing when I dusted, but it makes so much sense. Give your light bulbs and lamp shades a good dusting every so often and you'll be astonished at how much brighter the lights are.

Picking Up Glitter

We all love a bit of sparkle, but glitter is a nightmare to clean up – it gets everywhere! A great idea one of my viewers sent in is to pick up spilt glitter with playdough. Roll the playdough into a ball, press it into the glitter and it picks it all up. It also really gets into any crevices that the glitter might have lodged itself into. *Such* a good hack and as a bonus, you're left with beautiful sparkly playdough.

Moment for you

Master a New Skill

Is there a hobby or project that you've been wanting to give a whirl or start up again but can't find the time? Research shows that if you spend just 18 minutes a day on any discipline you can become better than 95 per cent of the rest of the world at it. It's known as the Rule of One Hundred – 18 minutes a day tots up to just over 100 hours across a year. Consistency is key.

So whether it's painting, yoga, knitting, crochet, poetry writing, photography, furniture upcycling or whatever else you fancy, resolve to get started. There are tutorials and how-to videos for everything on YouTube if getting along to an in-person class isn't an option. Good luck!

Final Word: *Trying to keep the house looking like a show home is as unrealistic as it is unnecessary. Our home is lived in and loved and happy kids equals a messy house – if they've been playing, running around and the place looks completely trashed, it's a sign that they've had a good day! And no one comes round to your house to inspect the dust on your mantelpiece.*

Hopefully some of the quick tips in this chapter will go some way towards keeping on top of the daily chaos, but do go easy on yourself.

Chapter 3

Household Sanity Savers

Scouring the internet, discovering, inventing and sharing simple but effective tricks for around the house is one of my favourite things. Whenever I find a new hack, it makes my heart leap! This chapter features some of the very best, all of which I've incorporated into our home and which continue to make my life – and hopefully now yours – easier.

YOU MAY NEED:

- Glue dots or museum putty
- Glue gun
- Double-sided grip tape
- Ankle weights
- Hanging hooks
- Binder clips

USEFUL TRICKS

Battery Test

If you're unsure whether a battery still has any life in it, bounce the bottom of it on to a hard, flat surface. If the battery is fresh, it won't bounce very well. If it's dead, it will bounce high.

Hammer Hack

I'm not brilliant with DIY, but I can hang a mean picture! I use a clothes peg to grip the nail in place while I hammer it into the wall to make sure I don't catch my fingers by accident.

Handle With Care

Let's be real: kids and ornaments don't mix. To help my break-ables stay in one piece, I use glue dots (or museum putty), which are double-sided and very sticky. I pop them on the bottom of the vase or ornament and then stick them down to the surface and they stay put, even if the kids are running around like crazy. Added bonus – they also make dusting quicker!

Removing Sticky Labels

I've seen so many people share different ways of getting rid of stubborn sticky labels, such as rubbing on peanut butter or nail polish remover and I've tried them all. The one I've found to be the most successful is to use a hairdryer to blow-dry the offend-ing item for a few seconds. This will heat it up just enough to be able to peel it back easily.

Easy Touch-Ups

With three very active children, it's inevitable that sometimes the paintwork in our house gets a bit of a kicking. I recently discovered refillable paint touch-up pens which make quick repairs to chipped or scratched walls faff-free. I've filled a batch of them with the paint colour for every room and they have a little brush on the end – so easy to use! You can buy them widely online and I keep mine in a kitchen drawer, all labelled and ready for action whenever needed. Which is often.

Noisy Cupboards

Take a glue gun or tube of superglue and place little blobs on cupboard frames to act as soft stops for the closing doors. Make sure the glue is fully dry before you re-close the door!

Repurposing Coat Hangers

You know those plastic coat hangers with the clips on either side? They generally come with online orders and they're awkward to use day to day. But if you remove the clips by sliding them off the hanger, you can repurpose them as clips for food bags. And the hanger left behind is now a much more clothes-friendly shape to use in your wardrobe.

Stop Slippy Rugs

If you've got a rug with no grip on the bottom, double-sided grip tape is your friend. It's so easy to put on – you can fix a strip on each corner or all the way around, depending on how much footfall there is. Pull off the other side and then stick down on the floor and your rug won't budge.

Ice Cube Your Plants

I used to wonder how I could manage to look after three children and yet struggle to keep a houseplant alive. I've learned not to over-water them and while it depends on the plant (check the individual care instructions), a good hack is to water them with ice cubes. Orchids, in particular, are kept quite happy with one or two ice cubes a week. The snake plant and cactus also respond well to this method. The ice will melt slowly, giving the plant a steady drip of hydration so that it doesn't drown.

Fake It to Make It

I absolutely love having flowers in the home; they really boost my mood and add a touch of luxury. But buying fresh flowers every week is way too expensive to justify, so I have invested in a couple of gorgeous artificial displays. They will last for years and all you have to do is dust them occasionally.

Buggy Trick

Have you ever been out shopping with your toddler in the buggy, all the heavy bags hung over the handlebars – and then your child suddenly decides to jump out? It tips the buggy backwards with a crash and sends your shopping flying. Put ankle weights around the front legs of the buggy and this won't happen again.

Scissor Kicks

Sharpen blunt craft, sewing or kitchen scissors with tin foil. Get a sheet and cut into it several times, completely closing the shears with each snip. Continue cutting until you're happy with the rejuvenated blades.

BATHROOM

Soapy Squirts

Kids tend to use way too much soap when washing their hands. To stop this happening, twist an elastic band around the top of the neck of the dispenser, limiting the amount that the pump can be pressed down. This has been extra important for my kids since lockdown and the emphasis on washing hands.

Foam Sweet Foam

To prevent your bathroom mirror from fogging up, rub a small amount of shaving foam on to the glass. This not only leaves it super clean, but also prevents it from misting over next time you have a shower.

Sweet Smelling Bins

Put a few drops of essential oils on to cotton balls or a few pieces of scrunched up toilet roll and place at the bottom of your bathroom bin to keep it smelling fresh.

Paper Stamp

This may seem a bit 'extra', but it's fun if you're having guests over and want to impress. Take the end of your toilet paper on the roll and fold each side inwards to make a point. Run your tap for a few seconds and turn off again, then press the pointy tip of the loo roll up against the spout of the tap for a couple of seconds (don't overdo it and let the whole roll become soggy!). Once the roll dries, it will be sealed with a 'stamp' just like the posh hotels!

Warmer Baths for Longer

On the rare occasions I get to have a soak in the tub, I want to stay in there as long as possible, so I keep the water warm by not skimping on the bath bubbles! Bubbles don't just make you smell nice, but the surface layer insulates your bath, keeping the water warmer for longer and giving you those extra minutes you fully deserve.

Too Many Bubbles?

If, however, you want to get rid of the bath bubbles, cold water does that really quickly (it might be that your child has added too much bubble bath and the bathroom now resembles some sort of 18–30 holiday foam party). Run the cold tap for a few seconds and they'll start to disappear.

Towel Storage

If your bathroom doesn't have a big enough rail for everyone's towels, attach a hook for each family member to the back of the bathroom door so the towels can hang there to dry and you always know which one belongs to who.

BEDROOM

Save Time Changing Sheets

A little sleep trick is to layer your little one's bedding from the mattress up like this: mattress protector, sheet, mattress protector, sheet. This will save you lots of time if you need to change the sheets when there are accidents or illness in the middle of the night – just whip off the top two layers and your clean bedding is already in place.

DIY Non-Slip Coat Hangers

If you have very smooth coat hangers and you find items of clothing keep sliding off them, use a glue gun or a tube of super-glue to put a small blob on the top of each end of the hanger. Let it dry fully (as with the cupboard door hack earlier, this bit is really important, for obvious reasons!) and then hang your clothes back in the wardrobe. The glue gives just enough grip to keep even the silkiest items on the hanger.

Bed Bumpers

Instead of buying expensive bed guards for kids, a pool noodle or even a couple of rolled up towels or blankets works just as well. Insert the noodle or rolled towel underneath the fitted sheet on the edge of the bed and make sure everything is tucked in securely. This will act as a bumper-like barrier and stop your little one rolling out during the night.

Pyjama Parcels

To organise my kids' pyjamas so that the matching sets are kept together, I make PJ parcels. Lay the top out flat and place the bottoms (folded length and widthways) in the middle. Fold the arms of the top in over the bottoms and then roll the bottom of the top up to the collar. Tuck the bundle into the neck of the top and it's a neat and aesthetically pleasing parcel! You can also use this technique with football kits and any other matching sets.

Stop the Stretch

If the necklines of your sweaters are pulled out of shape by coat hangers, try hanging them this way instead. Fold the jumper in half vertically so one arm is on top of the other. Place the hanger flat on top of the jumper with the hook end hooked underneath the armpits. The hanger should be upside down compared to the jumper. Bring the sleeves over one shoulder of the hanger and then the torso over the other. The jumper should now be wrapped around the hanger and is ready to put in your wardrobe. You can tuck the torso through the bottom bar of the hanger if there is one.

Ice Queen

If you have a rug with a curled up corner, ice cubes are the answer. Place a heavy object on the very tip of the offending corner to weigh it down and then leave three or four ice cubes on top of the area you need to flatten. Allow them to melt and for the rug to fully dry before removing the weight from the corner.

Do the Duvet Roll

This is also known as the 'burrito method'. Flip your duvet cover inside out, then lay it down flat with the opening at the foot of the bed. Lay your duvet insert on top of it, matching up the corners, then grab the top edge and begin to roll tightly. Adjust as you go, making sure that everything stays together. Once you reach the end and your bedding looks like a burrito, take each end of the roll and wrap the open end of the cover over the duvet insert, then unroll all the way to the top again. Sounds tricky but give it a go, it's really straightforward and excellent if you don't want to break a sweat making the bed.

Hanger On

Win back some precious hanging space in your wardrobe with a few ring pulls saved from fizzy drinks cans. Thread the hook of a coat hanger all the way through one of the holes of a ring pull. Then slip a second hanger through the second hole so the hangers are stacked flush, one sitting below the other. This will allow you to hang clothes vertically, instantly doubling your space. You can do this multiple times and have three or four hangers all attached together.

I also recently saw a really fun way of putting on a duvet cover which won't necessarily save you time but will give you a giggle. It requires two of you, so get your partner or other willing volunteer to stand up with their hands in the air and then put the duvet cover inside out over the top of them. They grip the top two corners while you hold up the duvet in front of them and get them to hold the top two corners of this as well. Go behind them and lift the duvet cover up and over the top of their head and then down again over the duvet and you're done!

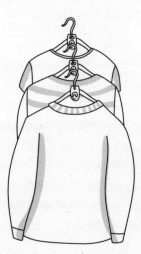

Throwing It Out There

I love having lots of cosy throws around the house, but I do have too many. There, I confessed. To give them another use, I turn them into cushions or pillows by laying them out flat and folding both sides into the centre. Take one end and fold down a quarter of the length – this creates the pocket. From the other side, roll or fold two or three times until you're able to tuck it into the pocket at the top and you can now display this as a cushion.

Secure Kids' Duvets

I don't know why this happens, but my kids' duvets are often found bunched up around the bottom of the cover by morning. What on earth do they do in their sleep?! To solve this, I lay the cover inside out with the duvet on top and then use small binder clips (the ones where the handles fold over) on each corner to hold the duvet in place. Flip the duvet cover over the duvet and you're good to go.

KITCHEN

Nifty Cake Storage

I'm going to file this under the 'things that are so simple I can't believe I didn't think of it before' list. Instead of getting leftover birthday cake all squished by closing a storage container lid over the top of it, switch the system. Place your cake on top of the inside of the lid and then pop the container over the top – it makes cutting slices so much easier too.

Nutty But Nice

The oils in natural nut butter separate and rise to the top forming a pool which can make it messy to use. To stop this happening, I store our jars upside down in between uses so when I turn them over to open, the oil isn't sitting on the top.

Keep Gravy Piping Hot

I use an insulated thermos for gravy to keep it hot while I finish off cooking the other parts of my roasts or Christmas dinner. You can even preheat the thermos by pouring boiling water into it first before emptying and filling it with the gravy.

Wine Time

Rather than standing all your wine glasses facing either up or down in your cupboards, store them alternating one way and then the other. This will give you so much more storage space in your cupboard.

Fantastic Plastic Bag Triangles

I fold all our plastic bags into neat triangles so they take up very little space – it means I can store them all in a small box rather

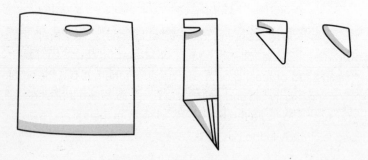

than having them clog up an entire drawer. Flatten the bag out, making sure all the air is squeezed out of it and then fold in half, lengthways. Fold again until you have a long, narrow strip. Fold the bottom corner to meet the other side, creating a triangle. Keep folding that bottom corner into triangles, left to right, until you almost reach the top and then tuck the end of the bag into the little pocket you've created.

Sweet Talk

To prevent brown sugar from hardening, store it with a marsh-mallow or half a slice of bread in an airtight container. They will both help it to retain moisture.

Cling Film Revelation

I wasn't aware of this myself until fairly recently and whenever I pass it on, people are amazed they've also managed to go through life not knowing. When you get a box of cling film, tin foil or greaseproof paper, it instructs in the small print to 'push in tab to hold the roll'. At either end of the long box, you'll find a perfo-rated tab, simply push them both inwards and they will grip the roll in place which makes it so much easier to get a cleanly torn sheet.

Better Binbagging

Next time you're changing the bins (which has got to be up there with cleaning the toilet in terms of my least favourite chores) try this. Instead of tearing off a new bag from the roll, put the whole roll in the empty bin and pull the top bag up. When that one's full, you just need to tie the top, tear it away from the roll and the next bag is already in the bin.

Moment for you

Homemade Face Mask

This is one of the easiest recipes I've found for a face mask and it leaves my skin super glowy.

INGREDIENTS
- ½ avocado
- 1 tbsp honey
- handful of oats

Mash the avocado and stir in the honey and oats. Oats have healing and moisturising properties and are good for nourishing and soothing the skin. The avocado will leave your skin silky smooth. If you don't have any avocado, substitute with 3 tablespoons of milk. I particularly enjoy using this mask during or just after a bath. Leave on for as long as you like and then enjoy the sensation of naturally clean and fresh skin once you wash it off.

𝔉inal 𝔚ord: *Nothing beats the 'eureka!' moment I get when I stumble on a new hack. It honestly never gets old. And then the chain reaction that sets off when I share it with other parents online (and in real life) is such a thrill. I love that we're all so connected and able to help each other both practically and emotionally. Keep spreading that joy. We all need it!*

Chapter 4

Getting Christmas Cracked

There's no doubt that Christmas with kids is magical . . . and, at times, unbelievably stressful! I love making the festive season special for the family, but I refuse to push myself to the verge of collapse in the process.

We've also got birthdays in September, October and December in our house, and it often feels like there's an awful lot of party and present planning to be done before I've even had a chance to think about Christmas, so I do try to make sure it doesn't ever become a mad rush.

Gift-wrapping hacks, DIY tree ornaments, clever storage solutions for decorations and homemade gift ideas all feature here, as well as my top tips for getting prepared for the holiday season so that come Christmas time there will be plenty of opportunities for you to sit back and enjoy a glass of mulled wine!

YOU MAY NEED:

- Sea salt
- Candy canes
- Washi tape (decorative paper tape)
- Plastic or paper cups
- Adhesive hook
- Ginger snaps
- White chocolate
- Coloured icing tubes
- Mini marshmallows
- Green food colouring

GIFTS

Present Planning

We all aim to give gifts that are wanted, but with so many people to buy for this can put you in a tailspin by December. I have a note section on my phone where I add gift ideas throughout the year as and when I think of them. There are also great apps for this like Google Keep, Trello and Microsoft To Do, to name a few.

Hark The Herald . . . Angle

I still get the same satisfaction with this one as I did the first time I discovered it. If you ever wrap a box-shaped present but realise halfway through that the piece of paper you have is slightly too small and doesn't reach over the item, turn the paper 45 degrees so that it's on the diagonal rather than the horizontal or vertical. Now when you fold the corners of the paper in, you'll find that you have enough paper to cover your gift – it's a Christmas miracle!

Ribbon Storage

A paper towel holder is perfect for storing your rolls of ribbon and is also easy to unravel and snip from.

That's a Wrap

Use an old suit carrier to put all your rolls of wrapping paper inside and you can hang it in a wardrobe, neatly stored away until you need it next. And it's also away from little pairs of eyes you don't want catching sight of it. Rather than securing rolls of wrap with an elastic band which can cause the paper to snag, use an empty kitchen roll. Cut the kitchen roll down one side and then place around your roll of wrapping paper and it secures the end in place, a bit like a napkin holder.

Recycling Christmas Cards

I use *this* year's Christmas cards as *next* year's gift tags. The small cards the kids bring home from school are especially good for this as you can simply cut them in half and add a hole punch through the picture side that usually hasn't been written on. Thread a strand of ribbon or string through for tying and that's it! I make multiple tags from the bigger cards and they look really good.

Candy Cane Sleighs

Try this if you're giving someone a gift voucher but want to present it in a way that's a bit more interesting than a bog-standard envelope. Glue or tape two candy canes underneath a gift-wrapped chocolate bar so they look like sleigh runners. Turn it over and stick a little chocolate Santa Claus on the top, tape the gift card to the chocolate and it's a really cute way to deliver your present.

Emergency Wrapping Paper

'Twas the night before Christmas . . . and you've realised you're all out of wrapping paper! What to do? I've been known to use tin foil a few times, which can actually be really nice if you add a bit of ribbon to it. A brown paper bag can give gifts a cool, rustic look or you could even use plain printing paper if you raid the kids' felt tip pens and add a few Christmassy pictures to it. Using a photographic spread from a newspaper or magazine is another option and sustainable, too.

DECORATIONS

Storing Fairy Lights

They look beautiful once they're up, but can be a nightmare when you unpack them, realise they were just shoved in a box last year and are now in a tangled mess. Argh! A great hack for storing them is to use an empty gift-wrapping roll, cutting a little slit in the end. Slot the plug end of the cable into the slit and wind the lights all the way around the roll. Cut another slit into the other end to secure them. You'll thank yourself when you're decorating the tree next year!

DIY Decs

You can make cute decorations by wrapping ribbon or washi tape (decorative paper tape) around Christmas cookie cutters. Add a length of ribbon and then hang it on your tree. This is a nice creative thing to do with the kids.

Creating a Centrepiece

Take some battery-powered fairy lights (you can get ones with timers so you're not running down the battery too much), a glass vase and some tree baubles. Place the baubles in the vase and then put the lights in too, spread throughout the vase and in between the baubles. I put the battery pack at the top around the back so I can switch off and on easily but it's still well hidden. This makes a special table centrepiece.

Smells Tree-mendous

We have a fake tree now which I find much more practical (and long-term use of them can be more eco-friendly), but I still want it to smell like the real deal. I found these fragrance sticks online which come in scents like pine and cinnamon – you just hook them on to your tree like a bauble and they give off a subtle waft of Christmas whenever you walk past. Alternatively, you could make some of the orange and clove perfume balls I told you about on page 37 and tie them to the branches.

Bauble Storage

Ever since I started using this method for storage, every bauble has survived from one year to the next. I use a big clear box (you can pick one up at a home/hardware shop) and some plastic or paper cups. Line the box with the cups and put the ornaments in them – if your box is deep enough you can make multiple storeys by placing a sheet of cardboard in between layers and lining up more cups.

Offer the Tree a Drink

If you have a real tree, then keeping it hydrated will help it stay green and lush – no one wants a withered tree past its best by Christmas Eve. A great way to water it is to use an empty gift wrap roll like a funnel so the water goes straight to the tree and not all over the floor.

Wreath Hanging

Stick an adhesive hook upside down on the inside of your front door. Loop a length of ribbon through your wreath and then place it on the front of the door and bring the ribbon over the top to meet the upside down hook on the inside. Once you've got your wreath in the desired position, tie the ribbon to the hook. You can still easily close your door but won't have damaged the front of it by hammering in a nail.

Snow-Covered Candles

Make your candles look really Christmassy by painting the sides with clear glue and then rolling them in sea salt, which creates this gorgeous glisteny, snowy effect.

FOOD

It's All Gravy, Baby

When it's our turn to host Christmas, I try to prepare as much as possible before the big day. And gravy is one of those things you can check off your To-Do list well in advance. I make a favourite recipe, freeze it in a sealable storage bag and then add the turkey juices to the defrosted bag on the day. It tastes delicious, but remember to take it out of the freezer in good time!

One-Stop Hot Chocolate Shop

If you've seen my Christmas vlogs, you probably know all about our hot chocolate station. It's become a tradition that the kids look forward to every year and it wouldn't be Christmas without it. I use a wooden tray to display everything: marshmallows, cream, mugs, spoons, candy canes and any other toppings. I use a vegetable peeler on a chocolate bar to make impressive choccy shavings to top. Here's my slow cooker recipe for the perfect hot chocolate:

Makes 8–10 cups

INGREDIENTS
- 250g milk chocolate chips
- 65g cocoa powder
- 100g caster sugar
- 1 tsp vanilla extract
- 250ml double cream
- 1.5 litres whole milk

Combine all the ingredients in a slow cooker. Cook on low for about two hours, stirring occasionally, until everything is melted.

Spreading the Cost

A clever budgeting tip is to start adding a few Christmas items to the weekly food shop a few months before the big day. So long-life products like chocolates, cheese crackers, drinks and snacks can be spread throughout September, October and November to avoid getting a giant bill in December.

Easy Peasy Christmas Pud Cookies

We love these in our house – they're so simple and they look fab. Take a packet of round ginger snap biscuits and melt down some white chocolate until liquid. Dip each biccie nearly halfway into the chocolate and then leave to set on a greaseproof paper lined surface. Once the chocolate has hardened, take a tube of red icing and pipe a couple of blobs on the white chocolate – these are your berries. Then use a tube of green icing to draw two little leaves. I keep the leaf artwork here very basic by doing one long line and then four little lines coming off either side rather than attempting an intricate leaf! They don't have to be perfect and they look so pretty.

Grinchy Popcorn

This yummy treat is soooo good for a Christmas movie night. Melt down about a tablespoon of butter and then add a cup of mini marshmallows. Keep it all on a medium heat until it's lovely and runny and then add in some green food colouring. Once you've got the shade right, add in your (ready-made) popcorn and give it a good mix around so it's coated in all the green goo. It's best to leave it to dry a bit so it's not so messy and sticky; I like to add in some chocolate treats as well for an extra special surprise.

Barbie World

If you have a gas barbecue, did you know you can chuck your turkey on it to cook? You prep the bird in exactly the same way as normal and put it in a roasting pan, but instead of cooking it in the oven, you whack the roasting pan on the barbecue! The timings are 30 minutes for every kilo and it frees up so much room in your oven for veg, potatoes and every-thing else.

Elf on the Shelf

I know the Elf on the Shelf phenomenon gets bigger every year – the videos I make of our elf get millions of views. If you're an 'elf house' but struggle to come up with a different idea every day, here are 24 to take you up to Christmas Day. They're all very easy and totally free, which is what everyone wants in the run-up to the festive season when we're time-poor and finances are stretched.

1. Draw glasses on the children in a photo frame with an erasable marker pen, with the elf next to it, marker in hand.

2. Create a 'Santa loves pictures, can you draw a picture for him?' station, with a piece of paper and a selection of colouring pens laid out next to your elf.

3. Have your elf create a donating station with a sign requesting that the kids choose five things each to donate to a children's hospital/charity.

4. Make the elf eat dog biscuits with a sign saying: 'Worst cookies *ever*, don't give these to Santa!' If you don't have a dog you could use something like crackers or rye crispbreads.

5. Pour a puddle of milk on to the kitchen work surface or in a frying pan with googly eyes, a thin slice of carrot for a nose, chocolate chips as buttons and a small ribbon as a scarf (like a snowman) next to a hairdryer held by the elf – he has melted the snowman.

6. Have your elf laid out on a piece of toast saying: 'I was cold but now I'm toasty!'

7. Wrap up their console controllers in Christmas gift paper with a sign from the elf: 'Out of use today, play with your toys!'

8. A couple of nights before, freeze a set of keys in some water – any keys, as kids won't know they're not your real ones. Set the elf next to the iced keys just before the kids get up and

leave a note: 'I've frozen your keys, I guess you're not going anywhere this morning!'

9. Have your elf 'decorate' the Christmas tree with everyone's underwear.

10. Set up an elf snowball fight with mini marshmallows.

11. Play a sticky note game by sticking different coloured notes all over the kitchen. Each child is assigned a different colour and whoever can grab the most in 30 seconds is the winner.

12. Have the kids wake up to an egg in a bowl with a sign from the elf saying: 'Sprinkle the egg with this magic dust and see what happens while you're at school/nursery . . .' The magic dust is hot chocolate powder and while they're out of the house, you can exchange the egg for a chocolate egg.

13. Write a poem from the elf: 'We left your dad a special treat, go find him and look at his feet . . .' Make sure dad's toenails have been painted – if he has socks on, it can add to the anticipation.

14. Put a new screen saver on their monitors or tablets such as a picture of them in bed at night with the elf, taken while they were asleep.

15. Attach a pink balloon to the elf's bottom with a sign: 'WARNING: don't swallow bubblegum!'

16. Have the elf replace the creamy middle part of a chocolate sandwich biscuit with toothpaste – he can be holding the paste and squirting it on top of an empty side.

17. Create a shoe train by making a line (the longer the better) of all the family's shoes, with the elf in the one at the front, as the driver.

18. Set up the elf to be drinking out of the maple syrup bottle or honey jar with a straw.

19. Have your elf playing noughts and crosses using red and green present bows on a board drawn on a sheet of paper.

20. Make elf snow angels using flour on the kitchen work surface.

21. Get your elf toasting marshmallows over an (unlit) candle with mini marshmallows and toothpicks.

22. Fill the sink with water and arrange your elf with other toys, as if hosting a pool party.

23. Prop your elf up against a wall like he's peeing and put apple juice in a small container in front of him. You could add a cheeky sign saying: 'Elf lemonade – £1 a glass'.

24. Have your elf create the sweetie rainbow trick from page 20.

Moment for you

Dedication to Meditation

Parenting is such a huge responsibility with so many demands. Meditation can be a brilliant stress reliever and also help you to increase your patience levels. If you don't know where to start, there are so many apps or free videos of guided meditation to follow and it can take as little as five minutes to restore some calm to your day.

- Allocate some time and keep it ring-fenced.
- Take yourself to a comfortable, quiet space (maybe this is best done when the children are out or asleep!).
- Shut or cover your eyes and notice what you can hear, smell, taste or touch.
- Breathe in and out slowly. As you do, repeat 'breathe in' and 'breathe out' in your head.
- If you find your mind wandering, notice and then consciously bring your focus back to the breath.
- Stop repeating the 'breathe in, breathe out' mantra, stay seated and still for a minute or two and then slowly open your eyes.

Final Word: *I'm afraid I don't concur with the classic Slade song – I definitely DO NOT wish it could be Christmas every day! I love it, but come the 1st January, I'm done and more than happy to pack it all away. I think it's so easy to get wrapped up (pun intended!) in pursuit of the 'perfect Christmas' that we end up running ourselves into the ground. Spending quality time with the people we love the most is what counts. And chocolate. Always the chocolate.*

Habits

Chapter 5

Chore-ganisation

We've hacked our way through the cleaning, laundry, rainy days and Christmas. Now welcome to the Habits half of Home Sweet Home – this is where I'm going to walk you through the practices and routines you can work into your life, which will soon become second nature.

If we didn't have at least a loose cleaning schedule to follow in our household, we'd really start to struggle. Having in place a plan which is shared fairly across the family really helps me feel in control and ensures everyone is doing their bit. Because being part of a family is about teamwork. We all have to muck in with the mucking out!

Speed Cleans

My approach to cleaning is divide and conquer. Trying to clean the whole house in one go is usually impossible and I rarely have a spare two or three hours to do this. Instead, I do regular speed cleans, setting a timer for 10, 15 or 20 minutes and seeing how much I can get done in that time. It's amazing what you can get nailed in these short bursts when you know you're up against the clock.

Power Hour

On the days I have a bit more time, I like to do a 'Power Hour' and really blitz the house in those 60 minutes. I'll always have a good podcast or an audiobook to listen to while I'm going, which not only makes the hour fly because my mind is occupied but also means I *almost* see it as 'me time'.

Podcast Faves

My favourite podcasts to clean to (because they take my mind off the task in hand!) are listed below:

- *The Diary of a CEO*
  I think Steven Bartlett is such a great interviewer.

- *Happy Mum, Happy Baby* I love Giovanna Fletcher and the honesty of the conversations.

- *Sh**ged. Married. Annoyed.* Chris and Rosie Ramsey are hilarious.

- *My Therapist Ghosted Me* Hosted by Vogue Williams and Joanne McNally, this one always makes me giggle.

- *Big Fish with Spencer Matthews* Spencer gets some excellent guests on here.

- *What'sHerName?* This is a Canadian podcast where they talk about women in history who did amazing things, but were never given credit.

The Top-Down Method

When cleaning, I always use the top-down method, which means starting at the highest point of the room, dusting the cobwebs and the tops of kitchen cupboards first. Then work your way down – cleaning the floor should be the last thing you do. This method will make you more efficient as there's no point in cleaning the floor first if you're only going to get it dusty again when you wipe the surfaces.

Pink For Sink, Blue For Loo

To make sure I never mistakenly use the same cloth for the toilet as I have for the sink, I follow this little rhyme. I always use cloths that are 'pink for the sink' and 'blue for the loo'. 'Green for clean' and 'yellow for dusting' completes the rhyme, if you want to colour code all your cloths!

Stack to Unpack

When you're loading the dishwasher, do so in a way that will make it easy to unload once it's finished. Stack similar sized plates together, divide cutlery into knives, forks and spoons and line mugs and glasses up next to each other. If items are stored in a cupboard to the right of the dishwasher, stack them on the right-hand side. Unloading the dishwasher has got to be one of the dullest chores, so the quicker you can do it, the better.

Delayed Wash

Lots of washing machines come with the option for a delayed start – I'd had mine for years before I realised this was a thing. In the evening, I load the washing machine with clothes, detergent and softener and then set it to start at 6am; by the time we're all up, it's ready to hang out to dry or to transfer to the dryer.

Before You Sit Down . . .

This is such a good rule to live by. In the evening, after you have put the kids to bed, don't sit down until you (and your partner) have done your chores for the evening. Spend 10–15 minutes quickly tidying the living room, putting the dishwasher on, wiping down the kitchen surfaces and when it's all done, sit back and relax. It's far better than the pain of being slumped on the sofa and having to get back up again because there's a dishwasher to load or toys to put away.

One Touch Method

I really try to stick to this because it works beautifully when you're in full flow with it. It's all about putting an item away with just one touch. If you're brushing your hair, rather than putting the brush down where you used it, put it back where it belongs. When you walk in the door, rather than chucking your coat down on the couch or over the bannister, take it off and hang it up in the place it lives. When you're doing your makeup or skincare routine, put the products back in their drawers and cupboards. When the kids get in from school, they should put their shoes in the designated area and hang their bags up. When taking dirty cups and dishes over to the dishwasher, complete the job and put them inside the dishwasher rather than on the countertop above it. Now there's a novel idea!

Delegate to Accumulate

Delegation is my favourite word. Delegate wherever you can. We got the boys to help with the cleaning from an early age, which has generally been very successful, bar the occasional whinge. At nursery and pre-school they learn how to tidy up their toys and it should be no different at home. Your little one might be very keen to have a go at mopping the floor or emptying the dishwasher, so let them. It teaches them important life skills, even if it takes you a little bit longer when they, ahem, 'help' you.

I also recommend giving children age-appropriate chores to complete. From the age of three we would get the boys to put their pyjamas under their pillows in the morning, clear toys back into baskets, put dirty clothes in the washing basket and hang their wet towels back up in the bathroom. Granted, I would have to fold the towels for them but they learned early on that we all had to do our bit.

From the age of five or six we'd expect them to be making their own beds, cleaning the sink of their toothpaste trails and keeping their rooms tidy.

Break It Down

Instead of saving up the big jobs for the weekends when we prefer to be out and about, I break them up and spread them out across the week. When it comes to laundry, for example, I do a load every day, putting it on in the morning as part of my daily routine so it's dry and ready to put away every evening. It makes it less of a burden than saving it up for several big washes over the weekend and I don't get The Fear from an increasingly bulging laundry basket throughout the week.

No One Leaves Empty-Handed

This is another one you can encourage the kids to take part in. There are often items which need returning to the kitchen or to their bedrooms, so before I leave any room in the house, I do a quick scan to see if anything can be taken back elsewhere. We also have a little stair basket which we can chuck stuff into ready to be taken upstairs. It means the stairs aren't covered in debris and it looks kind of cute too!

Keep Cleaning Products Handy

I know a lot of people like to store their cleaning products in one place all together, but I find that keeping smaller stashes in the rooms where they're used most means a cleaner house overall.

I'm more likely to quickly clean our mirrors, wipe down our sink or swish round the toilet if I'm in there anyway and the products are within reaching distance.

Here is a list of the products I have in a basket in each room:

- Bathroom: surface cleaner, mould and mildew spray, mirror and glass cleaner, microfibre cloth, cleaning cloth
- Main bedroom: duster, furniture polish, cloth
- Downstairs loo: toilet cleaner, surface cleaner, cloth
- Living room: mirror and glass cleaner, microfibre cloth, duster

The Five-Minute Rule

This is exactly as it sounds. If you spot a task that needs doing and know it will take five minutes or less, do it immediately. For instance, you might have a messy junk drawer which is the kind of job which is easy to put off, but will only take a few minutes to sort out. It's a very productive rule because it doesn't impact much on your time and is another example of how these incremental changes can add up to make a big difference.

Read the Label

We're washing and cleaning so often, most of us probably don't bother to read the instructions on the everyday products we use. But a lot of them, such as multi-surface sprays, recommend waiting for five minutes before wiping off. I spray and leave them to work their magic for a while and by the time I come to wipe, the grime has broken down and it really does make a difference, especially in the bath.

Be Kind to Your Future Self

. . . and tidy as you go. Don't leave anything until later if you can be doing it right now because you can bet your bottom dollar you'll forget and only remember when you're settled for the night with a cup of tea. If you can multitask, you will thank yourself later – for example, when I'm cooking the dinner, I try to make sure there's very little dead time, so I'll be washing dishes or wiping down surfaces in the gaps between. Even when I wash my face in the morning, I'll wipe over our sink with the other side of the cloth afterwards or when the kids are in the bath, I'll quickly wash the bathroom floor or organise the under the sink storage.

Get a Head Start

I'm not going to pretend to you that I get up at the crack of dawn every day, although if you are that person then hats off to you! But twice a week, on Tuesday and Thursday mornings, I wake up at 5.45am – an hour before the kids – and this gives me a chance to have a coffee, listen to a podcast, prepare for the day, perhaps get something in the slow cooker, edit some content or do a workout before anyone else is awake. It makes me feel so productive and there's something special about how quiet and still the house is before the morning chaos! I would say that if you have children under the age of three, you may find this backfires and they wake up with you, which obviously defeats the purpose, but now that the boys are older, this has become a really key part of my week and worth that painful first minute when the alarm goes off.

Words of Affirmation

The subconscious mind doesn't distinguish between what is real and what is not, so trick it! Repeating affirmations is a great way to do this: 'I am a loving and capable mum', 'I do my best every day', 'I am resilient and can handle any challenges that come my way', 'every day and in every way I am getting better'. Save your favourite affirmations in a list on your phone or in a journal and keep adding to and coming back to them.

Final Word: *Trying to keep a permanently spotless house all day, every day when children live there too is a lost cause. Life is hectic. You need a break. Remember that special word 'delegation' and make sure everyone under your roof is pulling their weight.*

Chapter 6

All Systems Go!

Our whole house runs better when there's a system and everything has a place. In fact, I love the whole process from the sorting out to the finished result. It looks nice and tidy so it's aesthetically pleasing but it's also functional and means you can always find something in a hurry because you know exactly where it should be.

Here are some of the best ways I keep our home and its contents in order.

YOU MAY NEED:
- Vacuum pack storage bags
- Label maker
- Open baskets (various sizes)

Organised Bed Linen

Bed sheets and pillowcases can easily get mixed up when shoved in a cupboard. Stop the muddle by folding up the sheet, duvet cover and all but one of the pillowcases and then put them inside the remaining pillowcase. The set is all together and you won't waste time searching for missing items when you change the beds.

Dreamy Drawers

Most people have at least one ridiculously cluttered drawer in their house! You know the one I mean, with what seems like a thousand little things all dumped in together. Adjustable drawer dividers or mini baskets are your friends here. Take everything out, get rid of anything you don't want or need and sort the remaining stuff between the baskets or dividers. When everything has a place, it's far easier to keep tidy.

While I remember, do measure your drawers and cupboards before buying any storage baskets and boxes. In the past, I've been known to steam ahead and have ended up ordering the wrong sizes, so make sure they're going to fit first.

Wardrobe Cleanse

Get into the habit of sorting through your wardrobe once every six months or so. Perhaps more often if you're a shopaholic. Take every item out of the wardrobe and divide into two piles – one to give away to friends, charity or the recycling and the other one to keep. My rule is that if I haven't worn an item for 12 months, I can be pretty certain that I won't wear it again. Sometimes I have to be ruthless, but I always feel lighter after I've done it and my wardrobe can breathe again.

Keep Track of Clothes

Once you've sorted your wardrobe out, here's how you can stay on top of it. Hang all of your coat hangers the 'wrong' way, set a reminder in your phone for six months' time and between now and then, every time you wear something, put it back the 'right' way. At the end of the six months you can see very clearly what you've worn and what you haven't and this will help you make decisions about what to cull next time you come to clear out.

Declutter Frequently

Doing huge clear-outs once or twice a year can feel very over-whelming and wipe out entire weekends. If you do it little and often, 10 minutes here and there, it's much more manageable. A good tip to help this is to keep a basket or box in a cupboard or in your car where you can put all the items you no longer want or need. Once it's full, you can donate them to a charity shop next time you're passing one.

Storing Seasonal Clothes

There's no point in having heavy knits and winter coats clogging up wardrobe space during the summer months, so if you have the space to store elsewhere, move them. I usually do this around the start of May when I can be pretty sure the UK winter is over and I won't be needing my cosy chunky jumpers for a while. I always keep a few sweaters back because the weather can be a little unpredictable though!

We're lucky to have a loft above our bedroom where I use big storage bags to make sure the clothes are protected from dust, but if space is at a premium in your house, this is where vac-packing can come riding to the rescue. You can pick these bags up so cheaply from pound stores and they work a treat. Just put your belongings into the bag, close it up and then using your vacuum, suck out all the extra air to shrink it right down. You can even make your own using a bin bag. Just fill up and then stick the vacuum into the top of the black bag, clasping the edges around it as the suction removes all the air. Once all the air has been sucked out, twist and tie.

I earmark a few hours around the start of October to swap everything back over again, ready for winter. I also keep my holiday clothes in the loft – things like kaftans and bikinis are only needed for a few weeks of the year and so they don't need to be taking up room in my everyday space.

Label Electrical Items

You probably have one or two areas in your house where there are a whole bunch of electrical items plugged in – behind a desk or at your dressing table, for example. It can be a real pain to know which plug connects to what item and you can end up disconnecting the computer when you meant to unplug the lamp. I use my label maker (any excuse to get it out!) to label each plug, but you could use a permanent marker or some stickers and a pen.

It's also good for phone chargers and other devices so you never forget which is which.

Keep Countertops Clear

There's something very calming about having a clutter-free kitchen and it also makes it much easier to clean. My golden rule for keeping the countertops clear is that if you don't use an appliance several times a week, unplug it and store it somewhere else. You'll love the new space you've created on your kitchen work surfaces.

To Have and to Fold

Store clothes in drawers by folding or rolling them into neat packages and then arranging them propped up vertically rather than placing them on top of each other. You'll save space, clothes stay tidy and organised and you can see all of your items when you open the drawer.

Between the Sheets

Keep bed linen in the same room as the bed it goes with, either in a drawer or a box under the bed. That way, the sheets won't get mixed up and they're right there when you need to change them. I also recommend having a good clear-out of bedding – you only need two sets per bed in your rotation.

Clear the Decks

Much like your kitchen counters, it makes such a difference having clear surfaces in the bedroom. The best way to do this is to give everything a home and keep things together.

- Fill a basket with your hairdryer, brushes and other hair accessories.
- Put all your makeup and skincare into a drawer so it's not cluttered on your dressing table.
- Clutter attracts clutter so clear your bedside table of anything that doesn't need to be there.
- Sort through the drawer space while you're at it. Your bedroom will feel zen again in no time.

A Basket Case

This suggestion came from a YouTube viewer of mine and it's one which I reckon will work in every family. She told me that her mum used to have a basket for each child in the house. She would put their clean laundry (older kids) in their basket, along with any toys or items that needed tidying up. Each child would be responsible for taking their basket back to their rooms and putting these things away at the end of the day. Such a great idea!

We also use big open baskets for most of the boys' toys, which makes it so easy for them to tidy them up quickly after playing. Just chuck 'em in, no excuses!

Rotate the Toys

Kids really don't need a lot of toys to entertain themselves – in fact, sometimes I find that the fewer toys they have access to, the more likely they are to play with them. But with all my boys' birthdays falling around Christmas, there tends to be an influx of new toys during December, so I usually put a few things away in the loft or a cupboard to bring out on future rainy days when they're craving something new to play with. This is a great space saver and I find it makes the boys really appreciate the toys they have. When I do it, I set a reminder on my phone for a few months' time to rotate again.

I also do a sweep of the boys' rooms every six months and anything they've grown out of or no longer play with, we donate to charity or pass on to families with younger children. I love it when toys get a second lease of life.

The 80/20 Rule

Apparently, most of us only use 20 per cent of the stuff we own which means we are simply storing the remaining 80 per cent. That's worth bearing in mind when you're having a clear-out as it might help you be a bit stricter with yourself. If you have trouble letting go of things with sentimental value, ask yourself four questions:

1. Does it hold pleasant memories?
2. Do I need this item to keep those memories?
3. Do I have the space to display it so I can enjoy it?
4. Would it be appreciated more by someone else?

The answers will help you come to a decision over whether to keep or part ways with it.

A Place for Everything and Everything in Its Place

It can be tricky to find a place for everything and it's something I struggled with when we moved house and started renovating, but I feel so much more organised when everything has an area to live. As you're going around your home, there are bound to be items which are permanently lying around looking a bit lost because no one knows where to put it back to or where it belongs, so create a place for it. Find it a home.

One In, One Out

Set storage limits for things. We all have a limited amount of storage space in our homes so it pays to be disciplined about this. If your wardrobe is full to the brim, you might want to introduce the 'one in, one out' system. It's exactly as it sounds – no new clothes can come in until you choose something to go out.

You can also extend the system so it means you don't replace anything until it's completely done or ready to be thrown away, like a new toothbrush, cleaning supplies and so on. Even better, switch to refillable cleaning products in reusable containers, which is far better for the environment and also means you never double up on packaging.

Sort on the Basis of Use

When reorganising the items you need to keep, think carefully about how you store them. If you have a bulky, heavy pot that you barely use in one of your easy-to-access kitchen cupboards, it's a waste of space! You probably have to move it to reach other things you cook with more often. Store lesser-used items in the harder to reach areas of your home and frequently used items in easily accessible places.

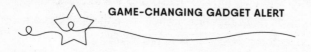

GAME-CHANGING GADGET ALERT

Label Love

My label printer is up there with my favourite household gadgets. You may know where every item is stored in your home, but chances are the rest of the family probably don't. Label your storage containers and the insides of drawers and this will help everyone in the house contribute to keeping things organised.

And Finally . . . When the System Isn't Working

If you clear out a cupboard, the hallway or a sideboard and within a fortnight it's a complete mess again, then whatever you're doing is not working. I have a strict rule with myself to go back to the drawing board for a second attempt at working out a system and organising a more thorough declutter to make sure everything has a home.

Moment for you

Photo Scrapbook

I enjoy having a creative project on the go that I can dip in and out of and develop over time. A scrapbook or photo album where you can collate your favourite family memories over the years is a really heartwarming project to get your teeth into.

Lots of apps will help you do this via a screen, but there's something a bit more special and personal about getting the pictures printed and then arranging those physical copies into a scrapbook or album yourself. Add a few notes underneath the pictures with the date, place and any anecdotes about that particular memory.

The Little and Often Declutter Challenge

If you're feeling like you've a mountain to climb and are unsure about where to start decluttering, try following my 28-day plan. Just 10 minutes every day and bit by bit you'll see a huge difference.

Day 1	Fridge and freezer	■
Day 2	Dry goods cupboard	■
Day 3	Two kitchen cupboards	■
Day 4	Two kitchen drawers	■
Day 5	Kitchen surfaces	■
Day 6	Under the sink	■
Day 7	Sort laundry supplies	■
Day 8	Clear living room of clutter	■
Day 9	File or shred paperwork	■
Day 10	Desk or work area	■
Day 11	Art and craft drawer or cupboard	■
Day 12	Sort all chargers and cables	■
Day 13	Under stairs cupboard or sideboard	■
Day 14	Medicines and first aid supplies	■
Day 15	Bath and shower products	■
Day 16	Makeup and toiletries	■
Day 17	Linen and bedding	■
Day 18	Towels	■
Day 19	Bedside tables	■
Day 20	Clothes	■

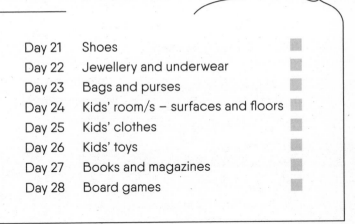

Day 21	Shoes
Day 22	Jewellery and underwear
Day 23	Bags and purses
Day 24	Kids' room/s – surfaces and floors
Day 25	Kids' clothes
Day 26	Kids' toys
Day 27	Books and magazines
Day 28	Board games

Cleaning Routines

Lean, mean cleaning routines for the whole family to help with.

SEVEN STEPS EVERY MORNING:

1. Empty the dishwasher if you have one
2. Put a load of washing on
3. Wash up breakfast items
4. Wipe down surfaces
5. Older kids to make their beds
6. Give the toilets a wipe (I have three boys, remember?!)
7. Sweep up any breakfast debris from the floor.

SEVEN STEPS EVERY EVENING:

1. Get everything into the dishwasher
2. Clear away the kids' toys, pens and books
3. Wipe down all surfaces
4. Clean the sink
5. Clear the floors and do a quick sweep or vacuum if you need
6. Put away any clean and dry laundry
7. Reset the couch and cushions for the next day so when you come down in the morning, the house looks fresh and tidy and you'll feel like you're already winning!

WEEKLY TASKS:

- Wash and change bedding and towels
- Dust household surfaces
- Clean mirrors and inside of windows
- Wipe inside of the microwave
- Vacuum all carpets
- Mop floors
- Clean bathrooms thoroughly
- Wipe down kitchen appliances
- Wipe down kitchen cabinets, especially handles

MONTHLY TASKS:

- Clean windows outside
- Vacuum under furniture
- Clear out the fridge and wipe down
- Choose a room or area to declutter
- Clean inside of the car
- Dust lights and hard-to-reach places

Final Word: *'Done' is better than 'perfect' and especially if perfect means driving yourself crazy in the process. This is something I repeat to myself often and it's a mantra that applies to pretty much everything. Lots of us have perfectionist tendencies but we don't have to be world-beating. Just getting it done is enough.*

Chapter 7

Happier House Moves

They say that moving house is the most stressful thing you can do and, having been through the process ourselves fairly recently, I reckon that's pretty accurate! Before this last move, Matt and I had only moved once, when we were in our early twenties and it was from a one-bed flat where we had so few possessions that we hired a van for the day and did it ourselves without breaking a sweat.

By the time we moved next, we had three children plus more than a decade of accumulated 'stuff', so it was a little more complicated and took a lot more planning. Before we head to the next section of the book, I thought it might be helpful to share some of the hacks which made the three stages of moving house – selling, the build-up to completion and finally move day itself – a bit more bearable.

Gosh, I was an emotional mess on the day we moved, I felt like we were saying goodbye to so much. Every single baby 'first' had been in that house. I even gave birth to Jackson there, so I found it difficult to pack up and walk away.

Thankfully, there wasn't much time to wallow! And by the time we woke up in the new house the following day, my sadness had been replaced by excitement about our new beginning and all the 'firsts' we'd get to experience in what I hope will be our forever home.

If you're going through this at the moment, I really hope some of the following sees you through.

Oh, and GOOD LUCK!

SELLING

Get the Price Right

Check your ego at the door and price competitively, especially if you want a quick sale. Listen to your estate agent – every street has a ceiling and they will know this better than anyone.

Deep Clean

Do a walk around and make a list of all the things that you need to clean and then start working your way through it. You might want to think about booking a window cleaner or carpet cleaner. And while it's not worth starting any major home improvement work, have a think about whether any of the rooms could do with a fresh lick of paint.

Take Photos

We took the photos for our house ourselves using a smart phone with a great zoom feature which makes the room look really wide. By doing the photography yourself, you can go from room to room and move any toys or clutter out of the way as you go, which would be difficult to do with an estate agent or photographer.

Personalise the Listing

We drafted a little bullet point list of all the key features in each room. Estate agents can't know everything about your home, so we made sure those details were included.

Put Rooms Back to Their Original Use

If you're using your spare bedroom as an office, put it back to what it was meant to be used for so your viewers can see it for what it is. In our old house, Jackson's room was very small and only contained a cot, so we decided to get a cheap single bed, which meant that when we had viewings, potential buyers could see a bed fitted into the space.

Viewings

If you have the time, do consider doing the house viewings your-self. No one knows your house better than you. We also held an open day, which got everything out of the way in one swoop and meant we weren't constantly cleaning and tidying for viewings across several days or weeks.

Staging the House

Go through your house and neutralise and depersonalise it as much as possible so the people viewing your home can imagine themselves in it. We took down some of the family photos because there were so many of them and we also used neutral bedding.

Tidy Cupboards and Wardrobes

No one is going to be cheeky enough to look in your chests of drawers or under the bed, but they may well open up fitted wardrobes and kitchen cupboards. Give them a good tidy so they feel spacious and clean.

Prepare for Questions

We were quite surprised by the number of questions viewers asked of us, so arm yourself with lots of good, upbeat and positive answers. We were asked things like: What are your neighbours like? Why are you moving? How is the parking? Where are the best places to eat and shop?

THE BUILD-UP TO MOVE DAY

Decluttering

Before you even begin to pack, declutter! The earlier you start doing this the better because I'm constantly baffled as to how we accumulate so much over the years. Break it down a room at a time and either chuck or donate. You'll find lots of decluttering tips in Chapter 6.

Take Photos of Your Electronics

Before unplugging your electrical items, take a photo of the back of each device so you know which cables go where when you set everything up in your new home.

Boxing Clever

If you're moving items yourselves, a guide I found online suggested you need around 10 boxes per room and then a further 10 as surplus. There's no need to pay for them – supermarkets and local shops often have plenty of empties hanging around and you could also put a shout out on your street WhatsApp group and ask your neighbours to save any boxes for you over the next few weeks.

You might find the freebie boxes don't have handles so use a craft knife to cut two slits into a 'V' shape and then fold inwards – I found this upside down triangular shape easier to handle than a rectangle. And remember to label your boxes clearly by room so you're not having to search the bedrooms for a frying pan.

Protect Your Clothes

If you're worried about any clothes getting damaged or dirty during the move, group them together in your wardrobe and then cover them with a bin bag from the bottom of the clothing upwards, tying the bag off at the top where the hangers are.

Parcel Tape

Fold over the end of the parcel tape every time you cut the end off. Not only does this mean you can easily find the end of the roll each time, but it will also save your nails when it comes to unpacking the boxes at the other end because as each strip will be folded over, you'll be able to find the flap of tape quickly to tear it off.

Shelf Displays

If you've spent time curating various shelves or other surfaces in your home and you want to set them up the same when you move, take some photos so that you can reference them and recreate the look for an instant home-from-home vibe at the new place.

Dismantling Furniture

When taking things down like shelves, beds or drawers, save the screws and all the other bits and bobs in a little sealable bag and tape them to the items so you don't lose them. Write on the bag what they're for and make sure you have some screwdrivers handy on move day.

For Your Buyers

Hopefully you'll still be on speaking terms with your buyers by the end of the process, so you might want to leave them a bottle of something cold and sparkling in the fridge as a gesture – get that organised in advance of move day. I also left a note with local information – our favourite takeaway, restaurant, café, things to do with the kids – and any little quirks about the house – so it's good to get this written in plenty of time rather than suddenly remembering as you're halfway out the door.

Book Removals if in Budget

We were planning on doing the move ourselves but booking an all-singing, all-dancing removals service was the best decision I made. If you have the budget for it, I can't recommend it enough. It takes the pressure right off and the speed those guys work at is a sight to behold. I don't know how we thought we could do it ourselves.

THE BIG DAY

Clean as You Go

As each room is packed up, take the time to clean it. I kept a basic cleaning kit to one side with a duster, cloths, sprays and a mop and gave each space a going over as it was cleared.

Keep the Vacuum Out

Don't let the removals pack this away as you'll want to give the place a final blitz once all the furniture has been removed. It's amazing what you'll find under beds – we found a whole brioche bun under ours. This also means you've got the vacuum handy for when you get to the new place and want to do a quick run around there as well.

Pack a Case Each

Make like you're going for a weekend away and pack a small case of essential items for each family member so you're covered for the first few days when you can't find anything.

For the kids I made sure they had school uniforms and pyjamas, plus toothbrushes, toothpaste and any other toiletries. It's also a good idea to pack some plates, bowls and utensils (plus a kettle and tea bags, of course!) so you can grab dinner and breakfast easily in those crazy first 24 hours.

Tool Kit

Have a box cutter and other tools ready to open boxes quickly and put furniture together without having to search through everything.

Document the Day

It might not feel like it when you're in the thick of it, but this is such a momentous day and one you will probably want to look back on once you're settled into the new place. You might be leaving behind a house with so many lovely memories attached to it and so in between humping boxes, take as many videos and photos as you can, even if it's just for personal use rather than social media. And don't forget to take one final photo outside the front door before you leave to mark the end of one journey and the start of a new chapter.

Final Word: Moving house is always a daunting task, but stay calm and keep using the 'little and often' approach. It's not a race and it's not the end of the world if you have a few boxes left unpacked. Take time to get used to your new environment and enjoy the opportunity to get organised!

II:

Food, Glorious Food

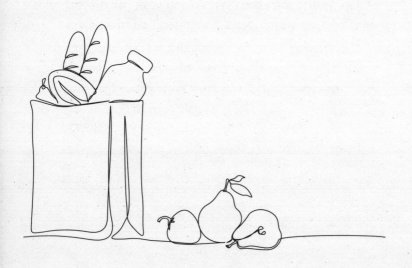

Making sure everyone is fed and that the food is nutritious and not something they're going to collectively turn their noses up at is a mammoth task – at times it can feel like you're the manager of a café with a posse of difficult customers.

Don't worry, I've got you! In this section I'm going to help you with family meal planning, batch cooking and slow cooker hacks. Over the next several pages we'll also be looking at quick and easy-to-prepare snacks that are yummy and fun. I'll share a fool-proof 'hide the spinach' trick with my delicious Green Monster Smoothie recipe, tips on how to keep a cut-up apple fresh as well as how to plan and prep so you never have a last-minute 'what on earth am I going to feed them?!' panic again.

Bon appetit!

Hacks

Chapter 8

Cooking Cleverly

Anything which speeds up the cooking and prepping process and reduces mess, I'm here for. Sign me up! Some of the hacks in this chapter are so simple, but they will all save you precious time and make your overall cooking experience, well, a piece of cake.

Measuring Spaghetti

You probably have a spaghetti spoon in your kitchen utensil drawer, but you may not have realised that the hole in the middle of it is actually for measuring the spaghetti! True story. Slot your dried spaghetti through the hole for the equivalent of one portion of cooked spaghetti, so you need never overestimate again. Now you know, it seems so obvious, doesn't it?

Spooning

I always thought that the holes on the end of pan handles were for hanging them up to store, but they have another function. They also provide a place to rest your wooden spoon while you're cooking. So, rather than putting the spoon down on the counter where it makes a mess on your surface, you can just slot the spoon handle into the hole and it stays propped at an angle so the remnants drip back into the pan.

Boiling Point

Did you know that if you place a wooden spoon on top of a boiling pot, it will stop the water from boiling over? I didn't until fairly recently either. This hack is mind-blowing!

Pizza the Action

When I oven-cook pizza, two won't fit on to one baking tray without overlapping. But if you cut them both in half and arrange them with the straight edges facing outwards, they will fit perfectly! It's like solving a puzzle.

Easy Ways to Chop . . .

PINEAPPLE

You don't even need a knife for this, although it works best with a super ripe pineapple. First, twist and pull the leafy top off the pineapple. Stand the fruit upright, lift it and then firmly tap it back down on a hard surface. Do this about 10 times, turning it round slightly with each tap. This loosens everything up.

Turn the pineapple on its side and roll it back and forth, pushing down quite firmly as you do. After a minute or so, it will be feeling quite squishy and the skin should be soft enough to break. Once you've created that initial hole, through the skin and into the flesh, it's easy to tear off the squares of pineapple by hand.

WATERMELON

The easiest way I've found to cut a watermelon is to chop it in half widthways. Then with the flesh facing downwards, slice all the way through both horizontally and vertically so you have lots of little squares. This makes it easy to pull out an oblong of melon, which you can eat just as it is or chop up into chunks for salads.

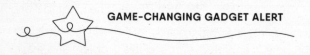

GAME-CHANGING GADGET ALERT

STRAWBERRIES

Strawberries fit into egg slicers just perfectly and the slices come out nice and even and look great served with pancakes or added to fruit kebabs.

One way to eat strawberries without wasting too much of them is to push a straw from the bottom and through the centre until it comes out at the top, popping off the green leafy part in the process (this straw trick also works for removing the stones from cherries). You can also buy strawberry hullers which are like a little claw that you stick on the top and twist off so you don't lose any of the fruit.

ONIONS

My husband Matt is very sensitive to onions and he used to wear a pair of not-very-stylish onion glasses to protect his eyes when cooking. But there is another way round this problem and that's to wet a paper towel and put it next to where you're chopping the onions. The idea is that the acid from the onions will be absorbed by the wet towel rather than your eyes.

GAME-CHANGING GADGET ALERT

APPLES

Our apple slicer is one of the most used gadgets in the kitchen. It cores and segments the apple in about half a second and I don't know how I lived for so many years without one!

GRAPES

Grapes are like sweets to kids, but they are also a choking hazard. They should be sliced in half lengthways (or into quarters for babies and toddlers). For a large quantity of grapes, I do this by laying them on a plate and then placing another plate bottom down on top of that to hold them still. Holding the top plate in place, cut through the middle with a large, serrated knife and you'll have a load of chopped grapes quickly! This also works for cherry tomatoes.

BROCCOLI

Cook it whole and then cut up afterwards – so much easier and less messy. You can keep the raw stem for smoothies and juices or for boiling up for broth.

Easy Ways to Peel . . .

GARLIC

The simplest way I know to peel a garlic clove is to cut the bit off the end and squish it down with the side of a knife. The skin just falls off.

HARD-BOILED EGGS

Place the cooked egg on a hard surface and roll it gently back and forth a few times under your palm. The shell will crack and then come away very easily when you peel it.

POTATOES

Boil potatoes unpeeled and once they're cooked, drain and leave them to cool for a few minutes. Where the skin has already split, pull and rub the skin apart and it will come off with very little effort.

MANGOES

Treat them like you would a banana! I didn't believe it would work but it does. Score the mango skin into quarters and then peel each section back just like a banana.

ORANGES

Use a small, sharp knife to score all the way round the circumference of the orange, although not deep enough to puncture the fruit itself. Then take a metal spoon and push the head of it between the skin and the fruit and work it all the way round until the peel is removed. I find this quicker and less squirty and messy than peeling by hand.

SHALLOTS

These things can be fiddly because they're so little, but if you soak them first in boiling water, they slip out of their skins.

GINGER

I love adding ginger to give dishes an extra punch, but it's so knobbly to peel. Using a teaspoon to scrape the skin off is quick and means you're only shaving off the thinnest of layers. It's also safer than trying to use a peeler or a knife. Whisper it, but I also love to cheat by using ginger purée or if I'm feeling *really* lazy, the pre-chopped stuff that comes in a jar.

Egg Checker

Eggs don't always come with a use-by date stamp, so to find out if they're still OK to eat, put them into a bowl of cold water. If they're going off they will float, whereas if they're still fresh, they will sink to the bottom.

Jazzing Up Your Cake Mix

You can make amazing cupcakes by tweaking a few ingredients in an ordinary boxed cake mix. Instead of adding water, add milk; instead of adding vegetable oil, use double the amount of melted butter; and instead of adding three eggs, add five. The cakes come out so moist and so soft, that they taste like something you'd get from a professional baker.

Smashing Mash

If you hate peeling potatoes, chop them in half (leaving the skin on) and boil as you normally would until soft. Drain and then place a cooling rack over a bowl and push the potato (cut side down) through the rack. The soft potato will go through to the bowl and the skin will easily slide off. You can then roughly mash a bit more before adding butter, milk and seasoning.

Honey Trap

When cooking with honey, oil your spoon first and the entire glob of honey will glide off in one go with no sticky mess left behind.

Sweetest Potatoes

For super speedy sweet potatoes, wrap in a soaked paper towel and put in the microwave for five minutes. They come out cooked.

GAME-CHANGING GADGET ALERT

Got the Scoop

I use an ice-cream scoop for my cake and muffin batter when dividing the mixture into baking trays or cases, which means they all emerge from the oven the same size. Plus, the squeeze and release action makes it really easy – no spoon scraping required!

Soft as Butter

If you're baking and haven't removed the butter from the fridge in advance to soften it, use the underside of a sieve to scrape the surface of your butter block. This produces finely grated softened butter, which is ideal for baking. Alternatively, pour boiling water into a glass, wait a minute and then pour it out. Place the butter vertically on a plate, pop the glass over it for a few minutes and that will do the trick. Like a sauna for your butter block.

Deeply Dippy Eggs

I find I get the best runny eggs by storing them at room temperature, adding them to a pan of boiling water and setting my timer for 5–6 minutes. By the way, I also love cooking eggs in my air fryer as it's so easy.

Clever Kebabs

Soak wooden skewers in water before using them for kebabs on the barbecue, so they don't catch alight. Even better, use metal skewers as they conduct heat and help cook the meat inside.

By the way, if you have a gas barbecue, you can check how much propane is left in your gas tank (if it doesn't have a gauge) by pouring hot water over the canister and then feeling it with your hand. It will be warm where there is only air, but cold to the touch where there is gas.

Keeping Herbs Fresh

If you buy fresh herbs but find they wilt away before you've had a chance to use them all, don't chuck them. I chop them up and then put them into ice-cube trays topped up with olive oil and store in the freezer to use at a later date for things like roast potatoes or chilli.

Another way to keep herbs fresher for longer is to stick the bunch in a little glass of water and put that in the fridge.

Prolonging Veggie Life

Similarly to herbs, in order to make your carrots, celery and broccoli last longer, chop the ends off and then submerge them in jars filled with water before placing back in the fridge.

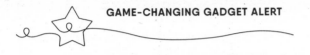

GAME-CHANGING GADGET ALERT

Drizzle Biz

I bought quite a few oil pourers online and they're great for both cooking and drizzling. They also make me feel like a professional chef! You can also just stick the spouted lid directly into the top of your olive or vegetable oil bottle in place of the cap.

Moment for you

Aaaaand Breathe . . .

This simple breathing exercise can help calm down a busy, pressured mind. In a quiet, comfortable spot, relax your facial muscles and hands. Inhale through your nose, slow and steady for the count of four. Hold your breath for a count of seven. Then exhale slowly for a count of eight. Repeat this cycle of four–seven–eight a few times.

Final Word: *In our house, the kitchen is the room we spend most of our time together as a family in. Finding hacks that help me keep things running smoothly there helps it remain the beating heart of our bustling home.*

Chapter 9

Snack Attacks

Straight after 'muuuuuuum!', the most uttered word in our house has got to be 'snack'. You too? My boys use so much energy, they seem to be permanently hungry, but I don't want them reaching for a bag of crisps or sugary cereal bar every time they have a gap to fill. So I make sure there are plenty of healthy alternatives in the house, often ready-prepared so I'm able to stay one step ahead and whip them out at a moment's notice.

I've put together a load of fab snack suggestions as well as tips on how to get the kids involved, give them some responsibility and make sure they're not constantly grazing out of boredom.

YOU MAY NEED:
- Freezer bags
- Black-coloured icing tube
- Cupcake cases

Fruit Loot

I like to cut up a bunch of fruit and veg, put it into an airtight container and store in the fridge so I can quickly grab it and steer the kids away from the less healthy snacks. To stop pieces of apple going brown, slice it into segments and hold it together while you secure it tightly with an elastic band – this will stop the air getting to it. Pop it in a freezer bag along with a little slice of lemon to make sure it stays fresh.

Eggs-ellent Snacking

Keeping a few hard-boiled eggs in the fridge is always handy for an instant snack and we have a constant supply ready in our house. Write on the shell the day you boiled them – they should be consumed within seven days. They're also great for days out and picnics because they are so easily transportable. Just make sure you store them in a cool container so they stay edible.

Watermelon Lollies

My kids absolutely love watermelons! In the summer, I chop it up into triangles and cut a slit into the green skin. Then you can wedge a lolly stick in the slit and it makes a cute party snack for a special summer occasion. You can even put these in the freezer to make delicious watermelon ice lollies.

Frozen Yoghurt Pops

You can turn ordinary yoghurts into frozen yoghurt lollies by cutting a slit in the lid, putting a spoon through and freezing. When you remove it from the freezer, run the pot under warm water and out pops a frozen yoghurt lolly. This is a delicious, cooling treat for little ones in hot weather.

Make Fruit Fun

When trying to get kids to eat healthily, presentation can be everything! I love making fruit fun by arranging it into cute shapes. There are lots of ideas on Pinterest – one of my favourites is a colourful peacock with half a pear for the body, blueberry eyes, a tangerine segment for a nose and a tail made with lots of different coloured fruits such as slices of kiwi, grapes and strawberries.

Fruit Kebabs

These are always a big hit in our house – I like to get artistic with the colours and make a rainbow or a sequence. Kids can either pull the bits of fruit off one by one or simply eat straight from the stick.

Homemade Trail Mix

This is so satisfyingly simple to make. Take a few dry ingredients like cereal, nuts, pretzels or dried fruit and put them in a bowl to mix. I usually add a handful of breakfast cereal, raisins, chopped walnuts, pumpkin seeds, popcorn and a few chocolate chips if I'm feeling generous! Store in a plastic container or glass jar, and when your child asks for a snack, you can just pour a bit of this into a bowl for them. Yummy!

Go Crackers

Take a cracker or a rice cake and add different toppings to dress them up. Our favourite toppings include nut butter with banana and cream cheese with cucumber. You can really get creative with these and make a little face with cucumber eyes and a cherry tomato mouth, for example.

Yoghurt Bark

Layer some yoghurt, 1–2cm deep, into a cake tin lined with greaseproof paper and top with fruit, nuts and honey. Transfer to the freezer until hard and break into pieces before serving. You can do this in a clean Pop It too if you put blueberries into the bubbles and top with yoghurt.

Squirt-Free Juice

Little ones often struggle with mini juice cartons – they instinctively grip them tightly and the drink squirts everywhere. To fix this, pull out the two folded flaps at the top of either side of the carton – they look like little wings! Teach your child to hold on to these 'wings' when they take a drink.

Cheese Ninjas

These are so cute and also something the kids might enjoy helping with. Peel back the wax strip on one side of the wax-encased cheese snack, as if you're opening it but don't take it all the way round. Then do the same on the other side so you have two strips sticking out to the side, still attached. Add two dots of black icing to the strip of cheese for the eyes and then snip the ends of the wax strips so they look like the ties on the ninja's bandana.

Snack Boxes

If you feel like you're forever fetching snacks for your kids over the weekend, get them involved in the process. Allocate a basket per child and fill it with their snack 'allowance' for the day. I like to add things like fruit, breadsticks, crisps and rice cakes. They can choose anything from the basket at snack time but once it's empty, that's it. This means you're only preparing snacks once a day, but it also gives your child a feeling that they have some choice and curbs the reach for junk food.

Shake It Off

I bought a couple of cocoa shakers for our Christmas hot chocolate station, but when not being used for that, I switch the chocolate for icing sugar. When I give the boys croissants for breakfast, sometimes as a special treat I shake a bit of icing sugar on top which gives their snack a finishing touch. Obviously this is quite sugary and so isn't something we do all the time – a sprinkling of cinnamon is a good alternative to have.

Smoothie Bags

Smoothies make such a tasty snack and are full of goodness, so I like to have plenty prepared in the freezer. Put all the ingredients you're going to need – veg, fruit, chopped up bananas – into a sealable bag, and then freeze. When you're ready to make the smoothie, tip the contents straight into a blender, add milk or water and you have yourself a refreshingly cold and delicious smoothie.

Butterfly Snack Bags

This is a fun way to separate two snacks for school or nursery. Put one snack into one half of a clear, sealed bag. Twist the bag in the middle and add a peg or clip to close off that section. Then put the second snack in the other half and close up. The two sections look like the wings with the clip as the body. If you want to go the extra mile, you can stick on some googly eyes and pipe cleaner antennae to your clip, but they'll still look like butterflies if you don't have these to hand! I fill these butterfly bags with strawberries and blueberries, or pretzels and raisins, but you could do them with pretty much anything.

Cupcake Sandwich

There's an easier way to eat cupcakes, which guarantees that you'll have a delicious mouthful of icing with every bite. Cut the cake in half horizontally and then put the bottom half on top, making a cute cupcake sandwich.

No More Sticky Hands

Avoid little ones getting sticky hands from ice lollies by using cupcake cases. Cut a slit in the bottom of the case and then slot the lolly stick through. The cupcake case will catch any drips and stop them running down their arm and also works more effectively and stays in place better than a piece of kitchen paper. The lids of crisp tubes work amazingly well for this, too!

Leftover Crisps

If you don't have a clip to hand but need to preserve a half-eaten large or sharing-sized bag of crisps, first push all the air out of the packet. Then fold down the bag as many times as it will go until it is just above the crisps. Pull both the corners round so they are on the opposite side to the roll and then fold the roll over the top and the packet will be sealed until you need to open it next.

Walk It Off

Do you ever find yourself getting sensory overload when the oven hood is whirring, the kids are playing with a noisy toy and your partner is asking you a question about dinner? Too much of this makes me snappy and sensitive, so I voice my overwhelm to Matt and tell him I'm going to take a little walk around the block.

Bring a set of headphones and plug into some music or a podcast if that's what you like, or just enjoy the space, the movement and the fresh air and return in a much better frame of mind.

Final Word: Mums need snacks too! So this one's for you and anyone who's a lover of iced coffee, which is one of my go-to drinks in spring and summer. Make up some coffee as you would do normally and then use it to fill up your ice trays and then freeze. When you come to make your next cup of iced coffee, you can add the coffee ice cubes without watering down your drink. You're welcome!

Chapter 10

Mealtimes Made Easy

I know only too well just how challenging dinner times can be, especially when you've got a fussy eater to cater for and trying to fit everything in around work, after-school clubs and all the other commitments and pressures we have to juggle.

Those 15 minutes when they're sitting at the table and you're fetching drinks, cutting up food and encouraging/pleading with them to eat at least some of the veg can often feel like the most fraught of the whole day. It's multitasking on stilts!

I'm always on the lookout for hacks which both relieve some of the mealtime madness and make running a busy kitchen much more plain-sailing and have found all of the tips in this chapter invaluable. I hope you do, too.

YOU MAY NEED:
- Cookie cutters
- Drinks dispenser
- Stick-on magnets
- Lazy Susan
- Air fryer liners
- Glass preserving jar
- Vacuum-insulated flask

Hidden Veggies

In an ideal world, our kids would happily eat up all the vegetables we put on their plates and then ask for seconds! But unfortunately, it's not always that easy – believe me, I know. One simple way to boost their veggie intake is to 'hide' them in as many recipes as you can. Add celery, grated carrot, spinach and onions to pasta sauce, blend vegetables into chicken soup – the possibilities are endless and your children will never know! Beetroot and carrot go well in smoothies and juices and veggie muffins taste great, too.

Keep offering them vegetables on their plate too, because eventually, if you set a good example, they will grow out of this phase. I've found success with raw veg and my boys love peppers, carrots and cucumbers with hummus over the cooked alternative.

Get Creative

Sometimes it's all about the presentation and I love finding imaginative ways of making food a bit more interesting for the kids. Arranging the various items on their plates into faces is usually the most simple, so noodles can become hair or grated carrot might become a beard with other veg positioned into facial features. You can even add edible food paint to make things more colourful. I've often used cookie cutters on sandwiches – we had a special dinosaur one specifically for that use – and at various points we've had crab croissants, bear sandwiches and bunny pancakes.

Food Spillages

We have a dog who comes in very useful for the inexplicable amount of food my boys manage to drop on the floor during mealtimes.

When we were weaning, the mess was on another level and at first, I tried using a mat. But that just created more work as the mat then had to be cleaned afterwards. A good tip for this sloppy stage is to lay down newspaper underneath your baby's highchair. Once the meal is over, you can gather up the paper with the dropped bits and put it straight in the bin or the food compost if you have one.

GAME-CHANGING GADGET ALERT

Pizza Cutter Cleverness

Use a pizza cutter to cut up your kids' food into bite-sized pieces. This trick works well for pancakes, waffles, toast, quesadillas and omelettes and it's so much faster to do one-handed if you're holding a baby in your other arm.

I also use a pizza cutter for chopping herbs when cooking and they're equally brilliant for cutting up an iceberg lettuce. Such an unexpectedly multi-purpose kitchen gadget, right?

GAME-CHANGING GADGET ALERT

Squash or Water Dispenser

My kids seem to have the impeccable timing of asking for a drink just as I've sat down to start my evening meal! Filling a drinks dispenser (you can pick them up at most big supermarkets) with water or squash before dinner means younger children who might not be able to reach the sink tap can serve themselves and without any risk of spillage. These are also good for summer barbecues when you have guests with children.

Designated Cups

Having a designated, easily accessible cup for everyone can really help save with the washing up. Magnetic cups that stick to the fridge are great or you could add a magnet to the cups you already have.

Conversation Starters

It can be hard to get kids to chat and I've learned that 'how was school?' doesn't elicit much detail. If any! A good conversation over dinner can help family bonding as well as providing a diversion from moaning about what's on their plate. Some starting points for this which are a bit more thoughtful than the obvious would be:

- What was the best thing about your day?
- What would your dream holiday be?
- What made you laugh today?
- If you could blink and teleport anywhere, where would you go?
- How were you kind to someone today?
- Who did you sit next to at lunch?
- What will you do to change the world when you grow up?
- What makes you happy?
- If you were stranded on a desert island what three things would you bring?

I also recommend getting a 'Would you rather' book, which is so much fun to play with your kids! We took one on holiday and did it every night at dinner and no one even asked for the tablet. Come on now, would you rather have noodles for fingers or 10-foot arms? It's a toughie!

Roll the Die

If they're refusing to eat what's on their plate, you could turn a frustrating situation into a game (and a lesson in negotiation and compromise). Make a deal that they can roll a die and whichever number is thrown determines the number of mouthfuls they have to eat.

Having said that, I don't think it's worth battling over this every time – rather than trying to persuade them to eat when they might genuinely be full, sometimes just leaving it is a good way of helping them understand their appetites.

Veggies With Screen Time

When the kids get home from school, I chop up some raw vegetables into sticks (carrot, peppers, cucumber) and serve in a bowl with some hummus on the side. The kids are usually tired after school and just want to chill in front of the TV for a little while, which can be the perfect opportunity to give them this to snack on. I find at this time of the day, they'll take what's on offer, especially when distracted by the telly.

Grazy Days

My greatest party trick: grazing platters! I make these whenever we entertain as well as when the boys have friends over or for special occasions like Valentine's or Halloween and they're so visually pleasing. You can make them either savoury (with meats, cheeses and crackers) or sweet (with biscuits, fruit and jellies) and they can be done at a low cost. A great way to feed a crowd without cooking and with minimal effort – here's how I do mine:

- Start by selecting a large platter or board that can accommodate all the items you plan to include. If you want to make a large spread you can tape cling film or a vinyl tablecloth to your kitchen surface and arrange your foodstuff on that.

- Choose the items; for savoury platters I like to add a variety of cheeses, cured meats, olives, grapes, crackers, hummus and dips. For dessert platters, fruit, marshmallows, chocolate-covered pretzels, biscuits and sweeties all work well.

- Start arranging the food with the larger items first, such as dips and cheeses. Continue to group larger items such as crackers (which I place stacked facing upwards) and meat together as it's easier to fill in the gaps with smaller foods like olives and nuts at the end.

- With cured meats I like to make meat roses – really easy yet sooo impressive. Take a wine glass and fold the slices of meat such as pepperoni or salami over the rim so that they create a layer overlapping each other all the way round. Add a second layer of slices on top of the first layer and covering the 'seams'. Continue the same process, adding more layers going round the rim until about the size of a rose. Then tip the glass upside down and gently wiggle it free and you'll be left with a cluster of meat slices that looks like a rose.

- Finally, arrange the rest of your items to fill in any gaps – you don't want any spaces left.

- Remember to be creative and have fun with your grazing platter. There's no right or wrong way so feel free to customise it based on your food preferences, dietary requirements, colour scheme and occasion. Enjoy!

GAME-CHANGING GADGET ALERT

Good Old Lazy Sue

I've got a few Lazy Susans in my kitchen cupboards and they are so handy. They are designed to be used on a countertop or table to distribute food or condiments easily, but I put them in my cupboards for all my jars, bottles of sauce and oils. Spin the wheel round rather than having to reach to the back or removing a load of containers before you get the one you want. You can even make your own using two round cake tins and a pack of marbles. Pour the marbles into one of the tins and then place the second tin on top. It spins around so well!

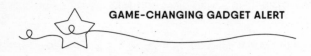
GAME-CHANGING GADGET ALERT

Easy Dispensers

When I shared the wooden dispensers we have for cling film, tin foil and sandwich bags on Instagram, people went mad for them! I picked ours up online and they come in lots of different sizes depending on what you're going to store in them. They sit really nicely in kitchen drawers keeping everything tidy and easily accessible.

Grab-and-Go Restaurant Bag

When eating out as a family, these are great to grab-and-go with. I use old makeup cases and keep them ready-prepared with things like little toys, crayons, felt tip pens and colouring pages to entertain the boys while we are at a restaurant.

Green Hulk Smoothie

If your kids are anything like mine, it'll be almost impossible to get them to eat spinach. One sure-fire way to get some green goodness into their tummies is to make a smoothie with cunningly disguised spinach. It honestly doesn't taste like spinach at all, so they'll have no idea. My youngest has been drinking these smoothies since he was two and he can't get enough.

INGREDIENTS

- 250ml milk of your choice
- 1 heaped tbsp nut butter
- 1 banana (I like to freeze any that are going brown for smoothies)
- 1–2 big handfuls of spinach
- 1 squeeze of runny honey (if you want to add a bit of sweetness)

Blend together until smooth and enjoy.

Fruity Smoothies for Fussy Eaters

It's not a perfect solution to the problem, but I find that adding a dash of sugar-free fruit squash now and again to a smoothie mix makes it a more 'acceptable' drink to your fussy eater. They're still benefiting from the goodness of all the fruit, so I'd chalk that up as a win.

Love Is in the Air

The air fryer craze shows no sign of letting up – ours was a life-saver while we were renovating. If you've cooked something sticky or messy, add some water to the tray with some washing-up liquid and then put it back in. Turn on the air fryer to a preheat for five minutes and it literally cooks the gunk off.

I also recently discovered air fryer liners and I really rate the silicone ones because they're reusable. If you're cooking salmon fillets, for example, put them into the liner and all the mess is contained.

Pancakes for Dinner

We do this at least once a month on the emergency days when I have nothing in or, to be completely honest, when I can't be bothered. Check out my Fluffy Rainbow Pancakes recipe on page 139.

Tin Foil Scrubby

If you have a pot that has caked-on, burnt food, but don't have a scouring pad or scrubby brush, scrunch a square of tin foil into a ball. This creates an abrasive, resilient scrubber that can tackle rice and lasagne caked on glass and metal cookware in seconds.

Perfect Picnics

LAYER SALAD IN A JAR

In a glass preserving jar, add your dressing to the bottom, then the most dense ingredients like sweetcorn, chopped cucumber, peppers and tomatoes with your lettuce leaves at the top. When you dump the salad out on a plate, the leaves won't have wilted, all the ingredients will mix and the dressing will go over the entire salad.

HOTDOGS ON THE GO

For a warm lunch on a picnic or trip, use a vacuum-insulated flask which you can put hotdogs in with boiling water. Pack buns and small condiments like ketchup and mustard (we save these from takeaways) and when you get to your location, you'll have a delicious hot lunch.

ICE LOLLIES

This is the hotdog hack in reverse. Use a vacuum-insulated flask to store scoops of ice cream or ice lollies and the insulation will keep them frozen for hours.

MUFFIN TINS

These are brilliant for holding drinks upright on an uneven surface like at a beach or in a field. You can also use them to put dips and selections of snacks in.

MAKE A CRISP PACKET BOWL

This is great for parties and picnics. With a large bag of crisps, you can fold the top of the open bag inwards a little and push up the contents from the bottom. Make it flat at the bottom by tucking the bag in on itself so it will stand up.

Potato Waffles in the Toaster

I promise you! Put potato waffles from frozen in the toaster twice through and they come out perfectly cooked.

Chilling Wine Quickly

I had to add this one here because it can be, let's say, useful after a particularly challenging dinner time . . . If you ever need to chill a bottle of wine that you've forgotten to put into the fridge, I have two ways to do this rapidly. You can submerge it in a bucket of water and ice and then add a big handful of table salt. The science behind this shows that the salt brings down the freezing point of water so your wine gets colder quicker.

Or, if you don't have any ice to hand, another way is to wrap the bottle in a soaking wet paper towel and then put it in the freezer for 20 minutes, after which it will be ready to serve.

Moment for you

Move More

I'm not naturally a 'fitness' person. I've never been good at sports, but after having children, I got into working out to try to lose some of the baby weight. Regardless of weight loss, working out makes me feel better and you don't have to spend hours in the gym. Just getting out for a walk can help clear a busy mind. I'm also a big fan of short HIIT routines, which you can find on YouTube and do any time.

Final Word: *I know how energy-sapping it is when mealtimes become a battle. Hopefully the hacks I've shared in this chapter will help alleviate some of those potential stresses, but try not to take it to heart if the kids refuse to eat a meal you've been slaving over. Remember, it's not a rejection of you but more a testing of the boundaries.*

One little extra tip which can make a huge difference is to say no to screens at the table. Putting the TV, phones and tablets aside promotes better digestion, more mindful eating and allows family connections to be nourished as well.

Habits

Chapter 11

Meal Planning Perfection

When I meal plan, I feel so much more organised. It saves me time and money and knowing that the mealtimes are all sorted for the week is one pretty major worry off my mind. So it's the ideal place to kickstart the Habits segment of our Food section.

I tend to plan from Monday to Friday and then leave the weekends more fluid so we can get a takeaway or go out to dinner and I always leave a bit of flex in the overall system in case, for whatever reason, we need to switch it up.

Whatever your situation – whether you work full time or part time or you're a stay-at-home parent – meal planning, batch cooking and finding ways to make your weekly food shop more efficient can really help to lighten the load.

I'm going to talk about all the above and much more in this chapter. Oh, and you'll find a suggested meal planner at the end.

Happy prepping!

Batch Cooking

In the past decade I've learned that batch cooking as much as my freezer will hold is a key element to successful meal planning. It's really straightforward: whenever I cook a meal from scratch, I double, triple or even quadruple the ingredients so that I can freeze portions for other meals on other days. It means there's a constant supply of homemade goodness available and if we have a mad rush day or after-school clubs, I can pull something out of the freezer and we still have a healthy meal with minimal effort. Dishes which lend themselves well to this are Bolognese, cauliflower cheese and fish cakes and you'll find the recipes I use for all of these, plus lots more of my family favourites, in the next chapter.

How to Meal Plan

You honestly don't need to be a naturally organised person to meal plan effectively. The more you do it, the easier it gets and these days it generally takes me about 10 minutes and then saves me so much more time across the rest of the week.

It can be done in four steps:

1. Look at what foods you already have which need using
2. Decide on which recipes you're going to make that week
3. Add any missing ingredients to your shopping list
4. Write your plan on a wall planner.

I do this every Sunday for the week ahead. We try to eat a couple of veggie meals a week and have fish on a Friday, which gives me a basic structure to start working from.

If your kids have a school lunch, look at that menu for the week ahead and check you're not going to double up and give them sausage and mash twice in the same day. I sometimes get the kids involved and ask if they have a particular meal they'd like me to include this week. This also gives you a bit of leverage – this is what you guys chose, so you'd better eat it!

Sharing Your Plan

Once it's done, I display the weekly meal plan in the kitchen, where the whole family can see it, but I'm always flexible with it and can swap the dishes around if needs be. Not ever having a last-minute hoo-ha about what on earth we're going to eat tonight is a huge weight off.

Slow Cooker Dump Bags

I love my slow cooker so much – it's easy to use and so nice knowing that I can put dinner on in the morning and not have to worry about cooking in the evening when things can get a bit chaotic. I've started making slow cooker dump bags where I gather together all the dry ingredients I need for various recipes and place them in a freezer bag. You can make a batch of these all at once.

I write the name of the recipe, the date and any essential cooking details (such as 'add one cup of water and cook on high for five hours') on the bag and then pop it in the freezer. Make sure the dump bag is fully defrosted before you empty the contents into your slow cooker.

Some slow cooker dishes which we find particularly mouth-watering include honey mustard chicken, veggie lasagne and chorizo and prawn paella. Delicious!

Keep Something up Your Sleeve

For the days when I'm rushing around or running out of fresh ingredients, I have a couple of simple recipes that can be whipped up using ingredients that I always have in. My go-to is a tuna pasta bake, which consists of pasta, cheese, milk, tuna, a seasoning sachet or dried herbs for flavour and sweetcorn.

One-Pot Cooking

I'm obsessed with one-pot cooking! Much like the slow cooker, it's so simple and there's obviously very little washing up, which is a big bonus. I've added some examples in the next chapter (see page 138).

Prepare Breakfasts Ahead of Time

Planning ahead isn't just for dinners, you can do it with breakfasts, too! American-style pancakes are good to start with – either prepare the batter and chill in the fridge, or make the pancakes in full, place in a storage tub and store in the fridge or freezer. When you're ready to eat them, just pop them in the toaster, add some maple syrup or butter and breakfast is ready. I also really love to make porridge or egg muffins in advance. There are so many options and it makes a change from the usual toast and cereal. You'll find lots of recipes in the next chapter (see page 138).

Meal Prepping

Meal prepping doesn't have to be complicated, but it will make you feel like Superwoman when it's done! Once a month or so, I'll set aside two or three hours to get a load of breakfasts and dinners prepped and frozen. In that time, I'll batch cook two evening meals – a chilli and a chicken broccoli bake, for example – and then, once cooled, I will freeze into portions for another date. With any leftover chicken, I'll make up some healthy lunches for me and Matt to have throughout the week so we can make good choices (which isn't always easy to do when working from home!).

During the same prepping session, I'll also get some French toast and pancakes ready, which can go in the freezer for future breakfasts. And, while I'm in the thick of it, it's also a good opportunity to prep any meals that are on the planner for the rest of the week – get the veg chopped, the meat marinated and so on. If you have older children who are confident with a knife, this is something they can help with.

It might sound like a lot of work (and it is!), but it doesn't have to be stressful and putting some music or a podcast on makes it much more enjoyable – you'll find some of my favourite pods on page 69. You'll have produced several meals by the end of it, and you (and whoever is helping) will only have one load of mess to clear up, which is a good trade-off in my book!

Chicken – The Gift That Keeps Giving

As long as you're not vegetarian, a chicken is hands down the best thing you can add to your weekly shop. You can get so many meals from one roast chicken and not a single scrap goes to waste if you use the leftovers to make delicious stock for the freezer.

I often put a whole chicken into the slow cooker. Brown the top of it in a pan or, if your slow cooker has a pan setting, put it straight in with garlic, a squeeze of lemon over the top (then push the rest of the lemon into the chicken cavity), 200ml of water and I also chuck in any herbs I've got going spare, like rosemary. I put it on high for four hours or low for eight hours and it's done.

Once you've got the meat off the bones, make your stock by putting the carcass, bones and skin along with some chopped veg into a large pan and bringing to the boil before leaving to simmer for a few hours. Strain through a sieve, cool and store in batches in the freezer for up to three months – you can use it for soups, risotto, stews and so on at a later date.

List It

I love a list. Even the weekly shopping list can spark joy for me! I've done our big shop online for several years now and it beats dragging the kids around the supermarket by a mile. Matt and I both have access to our account on the supermarket app and we both add to our shopping basket throughout the week whenever we notice we're running low on something. You could also do this with a shared note on your phones or a list pinned to the fridge or noticeboard if you have one.

Then I sit down on a Sunday night with a cup of tea, go through the contents of the basket so far and get everything ordered for the week ahead.

Shopping Smarter

I'm always looking for ways to make our weekly food budget go further so I make sure I check out the offers section on my supermarket app. If an alternative brand to our usual one is on offer, I'll select that instead.

When one of our weekly staples is on offer, I stock up, freezing the supplies if I need to. I also look at the cost per unit on items to make sure I'm getting the best value for money.

It's worth remembering that a lot of supermarkets offer a price match guarantee and give you money off vouchers in return.

Remember to use them! Or save them up over the course of a few months and use them all together for a lump sum saving.

Back-Up Meals

There will always be days when the meal planner doesn't quite work out – maybe you've been stuck in traffic and don't have time to conjure up what's planned or perhaps the kids have decided that whatever's on the menu that day isn't quite to their tastes . . . It has been known! So I make sure I've always got back-up meals in the freezer like sweet potato wedges, fishcakes, waffles, frozen peas and fish fingers, all of which can save the day in a beige kind of way on the odd occasion.

Example Meal Planner

Monday	Spag Bol (note: take Bolognese sauce out of freezer in the morning)
Tuesday	Baked potatoes and baked beans with raw carrots
Wednesday	Veggie pasta
Thursday	Vegan chicken pie and veg
Friday	Fish cakes and corn on the cob
Saturday	Takeaway pizza or leftovers from the week
Sunday	Roast dinner

Notes for shopping:
Don't forget to add corn on the cob to basket
Batch cooking ingredients for cauliflower cheese next week

Moment for you

Pamper Time

A bath can make you feel like a new woman! Do it while the kids are in bed, so that you aren't interrupted. Don't let yourself get side-tracked by a dishwasher waiting to be unloaded or an email that needs sending. That can all wait. Light some candles, pour in the salts, get rid of those annoying bath toys and add in some essential oils to make it feel like a spa. A neck pillow is a worthy investment for extra comfort or you can make your own by folding up a beach towel to the size of a 'cushion' and then holding the corners together with two larger safety pins or crocodile clips. Take two suction cups with hooks and thread them through the safety pins or crocodile clips. Then attach the suction cups to the bath in the position you want. Relax and let the stresses of the day wash away.

Final Word: If you've never meal planned or prepped before, it might feel like a lot of work at first. I promise you, once you get going, it will save you many a mealtime headache. And again, remember to enlist all the help you can get. Food should be something that involves the whole family as much as possible – it not only spreads the burden, but studies also show that children who help cook at home are more likely to develop healthy eating habits for life. Yes, even if they positively hate broccoli now!

Chapter 12

Easy Breezy Recipes

Sitting down together as a household for an evening meal is often impossible for busy families and I know it's not an option for everyone. Not many people's working hours are conducive to family life.

Matt and I are both self-employed and I know how lucky we are to have the flexibility in our schedules to allow the five of us to sit down together for dinner most nights. I value that time so very much.

I'm not exactly Nigella in the kitchen, but I have managed to build up a semi-perfect repertoire of decent family meals which everyone will eat. None of these recipes require a huge amount of time or culinary skill but they have universal appeal because they taste delicious.

BRILLIANT BREAKFASTS

Fluffy Rainbow Pancakes

Serves 6

INGREDIENTS

- 300g self-raising flour
- 1 tsp baking powder
- 1 tbsp caster sugar
- 2 medium eggs
- 1 tbsp maple syrup, plus extra to serve
- 300ml milk
- food colouring, various colours
- butter, for frying

Whisk all the ingredients (except the food colouring and butter) together then divide your batter into five bowls. Add a few drops of different coloured food colouring to each and mix (use a different spoon for each bowl, so you don't mess up the colours). Heat the butter in a frying pan; when hot, add a couple of tablespoons of batter for each pancake. Try and fit three at a time in the frying pan, and when bubbles appear on the surface, flip them and cook through. Repeat. Serve different coloured pancakes with bacon, fruit, maple syrup or any toppings you like.

Egg Muffins

Serves 6

INGREDIENTS

- 6 medium eggs
- handful of spinach
- handful of crispy bacon, chopped into small pieces (or swap for chopped tomatoes if veggie)
- handful of grated cheese
- salt and pepper, to taste

Preheat the oven to 200°C/180°C fan and line a muffin tin with muffin cases. Whisk the eggs in a bowl and season (if not serving them to babies). Chop up the spinach and wilt it down over a low heat in a large pan. Once wilted, add a tablespoon of spinach and a sprinkling of crispy bacon pieces or chopped tomato to each muffin case. Top up each with the egg mixture and a sprinkling of grated cheese. Bake in the oven for about 10 minutes, until risen and golden.

French Toast

Serves 1

INGREDIENTS

- 1 medium egg
- ½ tsp ground cinnamon
- 1 slice of bread
- coconut oil or butter, for frying

Whisk the egg and cinnamon together in a bowl. Melt the coconut oil or butter in a frying pan over a medium heat, submerge the slice of bread in the egg mixture then transfer to the pan and cook on both sides until golden brown. French toast also freezes very well – pop it straight into the toaster from frozen.

Apple & Banana Muffins

Makes 12

INGREDIENTS

- 150g flour
- 1 tsp baking powder
- 50g caster sugar
- 100ml semi-skimmed milk
- 1 egg
- 1 tsp vanilla extract (optional)
- 40g margarine or butter, melted, plus extra for greasing
- 1 medium apple, peeled, cored and grated
- 1 banana, mashed

Preheat the oven to 200°C/180°C fan. Grease a mini muffin tin with butter or margarine.

Sift the flour and baking powder into a mixing bowl, then stir in the sugar. Put the milk, egg, vanilla extract (if using) and melted margarine or butter in a jug and mix together. Pour into the dry ingredients, then add the grated apple and mashed banana and stir until just combined. Do not over-mix or your muffins will be tough.

Spoon (or, of course, use an ice cream scoop as recommended on page 107) the mixture into the mini muffin tray holes and bake for 20–25 minutes, until risen and golden.

Doughnut Bagel

Serves 1

INGREDIENTS
- 1 thin bagel
- 1 tbsp cream cheese
- 1 tsp sprinkles

Toast the bagel, spread on the cream cheese and then add some sprinkles.

Cinnamon Roll Smoothie

Serves 1

INGREDIENTS
- 1 banana
- 2 drops of vanilla extract
- 60g natural yoghurt
- ½ tsp ground cinnamon
- 75ml almond milk
- 6 ice cubes

Whizz all of the ingredients together in a blender until smooth and serve.

Waffles

Serves 6

INGREDIENTS

- 350ml whole milk
- 1 large egg
- 1 tsp vanilla extract
- 2 tbsp pure maple syrup
- 75g butter, melted
- 180g wholewheat flour
- 2 tsp baking powder
- pinch of salt

Preheat a waffle maker. In a large mixing bowl, whisk together the milk, egg, vanilla extract, maple syrup and melted butter. In a separate mixing bowl, stir together the flour, baking powder and salt.

Add the dry ingredients to the wet ingredients and stir until just combined. Some lumps are OK! Pour the batter into the hot waffle maker, one half cup at a time, and cook until golden brown and crispy. Alternatively, you could cook these in a griddle pan. Serve with fresh fruit.

Cool leftover cooked waffles completely before storing in freezer bags in the fridge or freezer. You can reheat these from frozen by popping in the toaster a couple of times (see my potato waffles hack on page 128).

LUSCIOUS LUNCHES

English Muffin Pizzas

Serves 2

INGREDIENTS

- 2 English muffins (or bagels)
- 2–3 tbsp tomato purée
- 50g mozzarella cheese, grated
- toppings of your choice (sweetcorn, ham, peppers, cooked chicken, etc)

Preheat the grill of your oven.

Split the muffins in half using a serrated knife to cut them and toast them under the grill until golden brown, or pop them in the toaster instead if that's easier.

Spread tomato purée on top of each muffin half, sprinkle grated mozzarella cheese over to cover and then add your topping/s. We love sweetcorn and ham, but you can also use leftover cooked chicken, peppers, pepperoni . . . the choice is yours!

Place under the grill and cook for 4–5 minutes, until the cheese is bubbling.

Frittatas

Makes 6

INGREDIENTS

- 1 tbsp butter, for greasing
- 2 red peppers, chopped
- handful of spinach
- 4 eggs
- dash of milk
- 100g Cheddar cheese, grated

Preheat the oven to 200°C/180°C fan. Grease a muffin tin and set aside.

Set a frying pan over a medum heat and when hot, add the peppers to soften. Next add the spinach and allow to wilt.

Crack the eggs into a large measuring jug and whisk, adding a tiny bit of milk if you have it as well as the cheese. Mix thoroughly.

Add about 1 tablespoon of the pepper and spinach mix to each of the holes in the prepared muffin tin. Pour the egg and cheese mixture over, distributing equally between the holes. Ensure you don't fill all the way to the top because they need space to rise.

Transfer the tin to the oven and cook for about 10 minutes.

Turkey Veggie Bites

Makes around 30

INGREDIENTS

- 1 egg
- 1 tbsp soy sauce
- 1 tbsp Dijon mustard
- 4 spring onions, chopped
- 500g lean turkey mince
- 2 carrots, grated
- ½ courgette, grated
- 3 tbsp flour
- olive oil, for frying

Add the egg, soy sauce, Dijon mustard and spring onions to a large bowl and stir to combine. Add the turkey mince and use your hands to bring the ingredients together before adding the grated carrot and courgette. Mix well and then add the flour.

Roll the mixture into bite-sized patties using your hands. Set a frying pan over a medium heat, add a little oil and when it's hot, fry the patties for a few minutes on each side (in batches if necessary) until cooked through and turning golden brown.

Bento Box

You can buy a bento box-style lunch box (with lots of little compartments) or use a few mini storage containers – I find it a good way of ensuring the kids get a balanced lunch. Here are a few ideas for what to include:

- Protein: hard-boiled egg/ham/chicken/fish/edamame beans/hummus
- Carbohydrates: breadsticks/crackers/pitta bread
- Dairy: cheese/yoghurt

- Fruit: grapes/strawberries/tangerine segments/melon/blueberries
- Veggies: carrots/cucumber/tomatoes/peppers/sugar snap peas

Pasta Salad

Pasta is so easy to customise to whatever you have in the fridge. If we have pasta for dinner, I often pop the leftovers in the kids' lunch boxes for the next day. Pesto is a super easy way to add a little bit of flavour as are chopped tomatoes with a splash of olive oil, then you can add any veggies or protein. Another classic in my house is pasta, mayo, tuna and sweetcorn.

Wraps & Pitta Pockets

A good alternative to sandwiches. For the wraps, put your filling on top, tuck the ends in, roll them tightly and cut in half. Some ideas for fillings include:

- Ham and cheese
- Chicken and cucumber
- Carrot, cucumber, hummus
- Tuna, mayonnaise, salad

For the pitta pockets, chop a pitta bread in half and fill! Great for little hands. A few filling ideas include:

- Falafels, salad and Greek yoghurt or hummus
- Cream cheese and ham
- Tuna, sweetcorn and mayonnaise
- Chicken and salad

DELICIOUS DINNERS

Quesadillas

Serves 1

INGREDIENTS

- 2 wholewheat tortilla wraps
- 2 tbsp refried beans
- serving of cooked chicken (I like to steam my chicken and this recipe is also great to use up leftovers)
- serving of vegetables (I like onions, peppers, sweetcorn)
- Cheddar cheese or mozzarella, grated
- salsa and plain yoghurt/sour cream, to serve

Take one wholemeal tortilla wrap and spread refried beans on to one side. Add small pieces of chicken and any veggies you have and distribute evenly across the beans (I don't bother cooking the sweetcorn or peppers if I put them in, but I sauté onions if I use them.) Top with the grated cheese, making sure that it covers all the veg.

Put the second tortilla on top and transfer to a frying pan, set over a medium heat. Cook until light brown on one side, then flip over and cook until the other side is light brown and the cheese is melted. I serve cut into triangles with salsa and plain yoghurt for dipping.

Chicken Nuggets

Makes 6

INGREDIENTS

- 125g rice pops or panko breadcrumbs
- 2 tbsp grated Parmesan cheese
- 2 large eggs
- 50g flour
- 3 chicken breasts
- salt and pepper

Preheat the oven to 200°C/180°C fan. Line a baking tray with greaseproof paper.

Put the rice pops into a food processor with the Parmesan cheese and blend. Transfer to a small bowl and set aside for now.

Put the eggs in another small bowl and whisk.

Pour the flour into a third bowl and season with salt and pepper.

Flatten the chicken breasts with a mallet or the underside of a pan and cut into even-sized strips. Dip each strip into the flour bowl, then the egg bowl and then finally coat each piece with the rice pop and Parmesan mix before laying on the prepared baking tray.

Transfer to the oven for 20–25 minutes, or until light brown and crispy.

Crispy Jacket Potatoes

Preheat the oven to 220°C/200°C fan. Prick your potatoes with a fork all over and place on a baking tray on the top shelf of the oven.

Bake for 1 hour or slightly more, until the skin is brown and crispy and the insides are soft and fluffy. If you're short on time, pop your potatoes in the microwave for 6 minutes and then finish in the oven for about 20 minutes.

Once cooked, cut open the baked potatoes and add your favourite toppings. We like:

- Baked beans and cheese
- Chilli and sour cream
- Tuna, mayonnaise, sweetcorn
- Cream cheese and spring onion
- Egg mayonnaise
- Coleslaw
- Sautéed mushrooms and garlic
- Prawn mayonnaise

Fish Cakes

Makes 10–12

INGREDIENTS

Fish filling:
- 800g Maris Piper potatoes
- 1 tbsp butter
- 2–3 x 145g tins of tuna (drained)
- 1 egg, lightly beaten
- 4 spring onions, finely chopped
- small handful of chopped herbs of your choice (optional)
- oil, for frying
- salt and pepper, to taste
- sweetcorn, to serve (optional)

Breadcrumb coating:
- 3 tbsp flour
- 2 eggs, lightly beaten
- handful of breadcrumbs

Boil the potatoes until cooked, then drain and mash with the butter. Season to taste. Add the tuna, egg, spring onions and herbs (if using) and combine well. Form into round, flattish patties and set aside.

Preheat the oven to 200°C/180°C fan.

Meanwhile, put the flour, beaten eggs and breadcrumbs into three separate bowls. Take a patty, coat it in the flour, then the egg and finally the breadcrumbs. Cook in the air fryer, about 6 minutes on each side, or lay on a baking tray and transfer to the oven for 15–20 minutes until golden brown.

We like to serve our fishcakes with sweetcorn. Once cool, these are great for storing in the freezer. Either defrost and follow the cooking instructions as above, or cook from frozen for 30 minutes, turning over halfway.

Slow Cooker Sugar Chicken

Serves 6

INGREDIENTS

- 4 chicken breasts, cut into chunks
- 2 tbsp flour
- 100g brown sugar
- 120ml hoisin sauce
- 3 tbsp soy sauce
- 2 garlic cloves
- 1 tsp ginger purée
- 3 tbsp rice vinegar
- 1 tbsp toasted sesame oil, plus extra for frying

Coat the chicken pieces in the flour and set aside. Set a pan over a medium heat, add a little oil and fry off the chicken pieces until browned.

Take a large bowl, mix together the brown sugar, hoisin sauce, soy sauce, garlic, ginger purée, rice vinegar and sesame oil and then add the mixture and the chicken to a slow cooker. Combine and cook on low for 3 hours.

One-Pot Bolognese With a Tangy Twist

Serves 8

INGREDIENTS

- 1 tbsp olive oil
- 2 onions, finely chopped
- 2 carrots, finely diced
- 3 celery sticks, finely diced
- 1 garlic clove, sliced
- 500g beef mince (or meat-free alternative)
- 400g tin of tomatoes
- 1 tsp mixed herbs
- dash of Worcestershire sauce

Heat the oil in a deep pan over a medium heat and add the onions, carrots, celery and garlic and fry off. After a few minutes add the mince and tinned tomatoes, sprinkle in the mixed herbs and stir to combine, breaking up the mince with the back of a wooden spoon. Reduce the heat to low, place a lid on the pan and leave to gently simmer for at least an hour, stirring occasionally.

Before serving, stir a few dashes of Worcestershire sauce into your Bolognese for an extra kick of flavour. This recipe makes about eight decent portions, so if cooking for your family, there will be enough to freeze for a later date.

Vegan Chicken Pie

Serves 6

INGREDIENTS

- 1 tbsp olive oil
- bunch of spring onions
- 150g button mushrooms
- 1 heaped tbsp flour, plus extra for dusting
- 600g Quorn Chicken Style Pieces
- 2 tbsp English mustard
- 1 heaped tbsp coconut cream
- 300ml vegetable stock (use a low salt option for younger children)
- a few sprigs of fresh thyme
- ½ tsp ground nutmeg
- 1 sheet pre-rolled puff pastry (almost all ready-made puff pastry is vegan)
- salt and pepper, to taste

Preheat the oven to 200°C/180°C fan and heat the oil in a pan over a medium heat.

Trim and chop the spring onions, slice the mushrooms and add both to the pan with the flour and stir. Once soft add the Quorn pieces with the mustard, coconut cream and vegetable stock and stir well. Pick the thyme leaves and stir into the pan with the nutmeg and a good pinch of salt and pepper. Leave to simmer.

Meanwhile, lightly dust a clean surface with flour and unroll the puff pastry. Use a small knife to lightly score it in a criss-cross fashion.

Remove the pan from the heat and tip the filling into an oven-proof baking dish slightly smaller than the sheet of pastry. Cover the filling with the pastry sheet, tucking it in at the edges. Bake in the oven for 15–20 minutes, or until golden brown. Serve with veggies or potatoes.

'Extra' Cauliflower Cheese

Serves 8

INGREDIENTS

- 1 large cauliflower, broken into florets
- 1 onion
- 200g smoked lardons (optional)
- 75g frozen peas
- 500ml milk
- 4 tbsp flour
- 50g butter
- 100g Cheddar cheese, grated
- 2 tbsp breadcrumbs

Preheat the oven to 220°C/200°C fan.

Bring a large saucepan of water to a boil and then add the cauliflower florets. Cook for a few minutes, then drain and transfer to a deep ovenproof dish.

Set a frying pan over a medium heat and add the onion, lardons (if using) and peas. When cooked, scatter evenly over the cooked cauliflower in the dish.

Place the cauliflower pan back on the stove, add the milk, flour and butter (easier if this is chopped into small pieces) and whisk continuously for about 2 minutes. The butter will melt, the flour will combine and the sauce will thicken. Once the sauce is nice and thick, remove from the heat and stir in half the grated Cheddar. Pour the cheesy sauce over the cauliflower and veg and then sprinkle the remaining cheese and breadcrumbs over the top. Bake in the oven for around 20 minutes until golden and bubbling.

This recipe makes about eight decent portions, so if cooking for your family, there will be enough to freeze for a later date.

One-Pot Veggie Pasta

Serves 6

INGREDIENTS

- 1 tbsp olive oil
- 1 onion, finely chopped
- 3 peppers, chopped
- 1 tbsp tomato purée
- 2 garlic cloves, chopped or grated
- 300ml vegetable stock (use a low salt option for younger children)
- 500g cherry tomatoes
- 350g pasta
- 100ml cream (or Greek yoghurt)
- 1 mozzarella ball

Set a large pot over a medium heat, add the olive oil, onion and peppers and cook for about 5 minutes, stirring occasionally. Add the tomato purée, garlic and stock and stir. Chuck in the cherry tomatoes and pasta and let the whole thing bubble and cook for about 15 minutes.

When the pasta is ready, stir in the cream or Greek yoghurt and tear in the mozzarella. Stir one last time until combined and serve.

Be a Bookworm

I adore books but struggle to sit down and read for a long period of time. Often, when I try to read in bed, I fall asleep after two pages! I've mentioned before that audiobooks have been a revelation for me because I can listen while getting various chores done or walking to the shops or to pick the boys up.

I have a library on my phone which I keep adding to on recommendations and I love having a stack to work my way through. If you also find it difficult to find the time to read, try downloading an audiobook and see if it could work for you too.

And if you've got a group of friends who also love to read, think about setting up an informal book group where you all pick the same novel and then meet up every four to six weeks to discuss and dissect it.

Final Word: *Hopefully there is enough variety here to keep even the fussiest of palates happy – I know that finding a recipe everyone in the family enjoys is like gold dust! But trying to cook everything from scratch is not always possible so make sure you whip out the tried and tested beans on toast or fish fingers and waffles, too. Life is all about balance, right?*

III:

Travel & Holidays

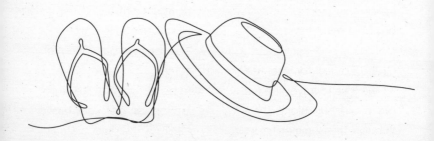

During the summer break we need all the help we can get. The six-week stretch is a daunting prospect for many of us who find ourselves scrambling around for childcare 'solutions' which will almost certainly not fit around our working hours, but will very definitely put a dent in our bank accounts.

As 50 per cent of UK families now have two parents working full-time, the summer struggle is real and it's hardly surprising that it can push people to breaking point.

A week or two away is always lovely, but even that presents challenges aplenty and keeping the children entertained, hydrated and enjoying the sun safely is not a challenge for the fainthearted! Throw in travel sickness and boredom, along with a million things to pack and logistics to figure out and it can all become quite the headache. Especially when you're stuck on a motorway and you've sung 'The Wheels on the Bus' and 'Ten Green Bottles' for what feels like an eternity.

We love to travel as a family, but we'd be lost without the hacks I've picked up along the way. This section will get your family through the summer happily and healthily, with some beautiful memories to boot. I've covered everything including beach hacks, packing tips and a guaranteed survival plan for those long journeys. Buckle up!

Hacks

Chapter 13

Planes, Trains & Automobiles

If I could invent one thing, it would be a teleporter which would get us all from A to B in an instant, without the journey in between. Just imagine! But in the absence of that, here is my advice (informed by lived experience!) for getting through the flight, train ride or long drive up the motorway in one piece. Spoiler alert: pack snacks . . .

YOU MAY NEED:
- Cereal dispenser
- Dog seat cover
- Suction grip shower caddy
- Car seat tray

CARS

Bin It!

I probably should have banned food from my car years ago, but here we are. Kids plus journeys of any length equals a demand for snacks. And snacks mean empty wrappers and cartons littered all over the backseat.

Minimise mess in the car by taking an old plastic cereal dispenser (you could line it with a plastic bag if you wanted to) and get the kids to 'post' all their rubbish in there – they can empty it out themselves at the end of the journey. These containers are especially nifty because they have a lid to keep the debris contained.

Travel Sickness Solutions

One of my boys can get very travel sick and so, after years of having a bowl in the car, I finally ordered some actual travel sickness bags online. If your child is ill, you can dispose of the, er, deposit easily, so it's great to have a few of these on hand for every journey.

Protecting Car Seats

A fab solution for accidental spillages (and worse) is a washable dog seat cover which stretches right across the back of the car. I cut holes for the seatbelts so all the safety buckles still connect.

Over-the-Seat Storage

Storing all the things that your children are going to need for the car journey so it's accessible to them is a no-brainer for me. You can pick up these organisers really cheaply and they just hang over the back of the seat in front of the kids. Load them up with anything they're going to play with, plus any drinks, snacks (always the snacks!) pens and books or comics. The ones we have even have a space for a tablet so they can watch a movie you've downloaded hands-free. It also means you're not constantly having to rummage around your feet in the front trying to find whatever it is they're wanting now . . .

Window Shower Caddy

If your little ones can't quite reach the back of the seat in front of them, pick up a basic shower caddy with suction cups on the back. Fill it up with things like colouring pens, paper, a bottle of water and stick it to the inside window so they can easily get to it.

GAME-CHANGING GADGET ALERT

Lap Tray

This is such a clever little invention and we've had good use out of ours over the years. It's a tray which sits on their lap and provides a space where they can play with their toys or do their colouring in. Ours even came with marker pens and the tray itself is a whiteboard so they can use that to draw on. It holds little toys really well and you don't have to just use it in the car – we often used ours with the buggy or attached it to a chair in the house.

You could make your own using an ordinary plastic tray and attaching a cushion to the underneath for comfort and stability. A white surface tray will allow them to draw on it and wipe clean.

Multi-Cup Holder

Our car doesn't have enough cup holders for all five of us, so I bought a multi-cup holder which can carry up to four cups or bottles. It means we can easily transport our water, juice and the all-important coffee.

Audiobook Heroes

Reading or looking at screens in the car can bring on travel sickness so we've found that audiobooks provide welcome entertainment and distraction during the journey. I download a decent selection for each child before we set off and they listen to them with headphones while looking out the window and watching the world go by.

Travel Bingo

Always such a hit with our kids! Print off a few different versions of travel bingo online or you could easily make your own and it's a fab game to play when you're on the road. Each time they spot something on their bingo card – it could be things like a caravan, a wind turbine, a petrol station and so on – they tick it off. I like to throw in a few obscure ones such as a horsebox and a yellow car (more unusual than you might think!) to make sure the game keeps them occupied. This can also work on trains if you adapt the items to suit. So for example: horses, cows, a tractor, the ticket inspector and another train passing by are all good for this.

Spot the Mini

On a similar theme to the bingo, we play this game which means whenever you spot a Mini, the first to shout out gets a point. And if you see a yellow Mini that's an instant win. A Mini is a good car to choose because they're rare enough for it to be a challenge, but not so rare that you're never going to spot any at all. Matt admitted to me recently that he even plays this on his own, shouting out 'Mini!' to an empty car!

Map Out the Journey

There's nothing worse than a constant chorus of 'are we nearly there yet?' on a long car journey, especially when it begins three minutes after setting off. One good hack is to print off (or draw if you're feeling artistic) a map of the journey, put it in a plastic wallet and hang it on the back of one of the front seats so that the kids can see it. You could include stop off points, and how long each part of the journey will take. My eldest son enjoys ticking off places as we pass them, so it's good fun and great for teaching the kids a bit of geography, too!

Kitted Out

Lots of cars come with their own first aid kit these days and in many European countries it's compulsory to travel with one. I'd recommend keeping one in your vehicle at all times – you can pick one up online or make your own with things you know your family might need or will definitely use when you go away. I have a vanity case with pain relief for kids, allergy tablets, wound wash, plasters, antiseptic cream, paracetamol, bandages and barrier cream.

Telling Tales

I saw a tip online about car journeys that I thought sounded fun. If you pick another car with a family in it who are travelling along the same road, ask the kids to create a story around them. Where are they going? Where do they live? What are their names? What do they like doing? Again, it's good to stoke up a bit of imagination.

Steamy Windows

Nothing to do with the kids, but here's a nice one for whoever is the designated driver. If you smear a pea-sized amount of toothpaste on your wing mirrors and then buff them with a clean cloth, it forms an invisible barrier which means they will never get foggy when covered in raindrops on a wet day. How clever!

AEROPLANES

Pens on a String

I love these so much! It's such a simple invention but feels revolutionary – a bunch of felt tip pens which come with a loop in the cap so they can all be joined together on a large ring. Brilliant. Never lose a pen top again – hurrah.

Loadsa Lego

I always bring a freezer bag full of Lego to keep the kids entertained on long flights or train journeys. You can even make your own portable Lego table by gluing a flat Lego base to a small tray which can sit across their lap and gives them a base to build from.

Mile-High Cinema

Create an in-flight movie theatre by popping their tablets or your phone into a clear bag from airport security and then pinning it to the seat in front using the table clip. They can watch whatever you've downloaded for them while snuggled up or having a snack.

Changing Nappies on the Go

For very little ones, I always packed one nappy per hour of travel, so if we were going on a five-hour flight, I'd pack eight nappies to include the three hours at the airport. This may seem excessive, but rather that than the alternative!

Backpack Hack

Use a backpack as a carry-on when children are young instead of a suitcase or over-the-shoulder bag. It allows you to have both hands free to manage the kids and all their belongings and is easier for you when tired legs need a carry.

Comfort Is Key

When flying with older children, a blanket and travel pillow can really help on a long flight. I pack these under the chair in front of them, or at their feet so that they can reach them.

We also used a little travel bed when the boys were toddlers, which is just an inflatable footrest that fits on to the end of their chair.

TRAINS

Nabbing Seats

Because under-fives travel free on most journeys, that also means train companies won't allocate them a seat. Not exactly practical. A top tip for making sure you've all got somewhere to sit, is to find out from a guard on the platform before the train arrives which carriage has the unreserved seating and where you should stand to board that carriage first. That useful intel should mean that as soon as the train doors open, you can make a bee-line for an empty table seat and won't have to spend the journey wrestling with a toddler on your lap.

Efficient Arrivals

When on a train, set an alert on your phone for about 15 minutes before your stop and start gathering up and packing away all the pens, books, tablets etc, especially if it's going on elsewhere and you'll have a limited amount of time to get off. Avoid a last-minute dash to disembark at all costs and check under the table and the seats before you leave!

Triangular Crayons

It's all fun and games with crayons but they are constantly rolling on to the floor, especially on a moving train. I found some tri-angular non-roll crayons and think they are such a good solution to a very annoying problem!

On the Cards

Take a pack of cards! Never has an item so compact possessed so many possibilities. Other small but perfectly formed games for on the go include Uno, Dobble, Sushi Go and Sleeping Queens.

Playing Consequences

This is a game of creativity, imagination and storytelling for older children who can read and write and it's great for train journeys. Each player is given a piece of A4 paper which they fold into eight horizontal sections. To start the game, everyone writes the name of a famous male or male friend or family member in the top section and folds it over so no one can see what they've written. Everyone then passes their sheet of paper to the next player.

The rest of the game goes as follows with each section folded over and passed along:

'Met': (famous female or female friend or family member)

'In/At/On': (place where they met)

'He said to her':

'She said to him':

'He': (what he did)

'Then she': (what she did)

'And the consequence was': (how the story concludes)

When you read out the full stories at the end, it often produces hilarious results ranging from the sublime to the ridiculous and it whiles away the time quite brilliantly.

Cold Shower

OK, bear with me on this one because I realise that this does not sound like a 'moment' that you will enjoy. But switching the tap at the end of your shower to blast freezing cold water for 30 seconds (or as long as you can stand!) has so many health benefits. Exposure to the cold triggers the release of endorphins and dopamine, which are natural mood boosters. It can also improve circulation, reduce stress and it'll certainly wake up tired limbs and minds.

Final Word: *What's that saying? It's not about the destination, it's about the journey . . . Yeah, maybe not when you're travelling with kids! Seriously though, the journey can become part of the adventure and just as memory-making as the holiday itself. Safe travels!*

Chapter 14

Just Beachy

Before having children, a day at the beach would mean packing a small bag with a book, sun cream and a towel and off I'd go, footloose and fancy free. Not anymore! Memory-making beach days with the kids are lovely and we always have such an awesome time, but it does take some planning . . . and a considerably bigger bag!

YOU MAY NEED:
- Old shower curtain
- Talcum powder
- Fitted sheet
- Mesh bags

Make Your Own Paddling Pool

When my boys were younger and we were on the beach, I'd worry about them going in the sea because of the current. So I would make an alternative pool to paddle in away from the shore by digging a shallow hole in the sand and lining it with a shower curtain or waterproof tablecloth. Pat the sand down around the edges to weigh down the sides, fill it up with water and you've got a safe 'sea' to splash about in.

Talc in a Sock

Use ordinary talcum powder to get all the sand off feet, hands and bodies. Put the talc in a sock first – this is much less messy than pouring directly from the bottle to the skin because the powder passes through the small holes in the fabric – and dust all over your sandy bits. A quick rub with a towel afterwards and the sand disappears. This is particularly good for those pesky in-between-the-toes areas!

Easy-On Sun Cream

One of my viewers sent me this hack, and it really works! If your child is fussy when you try to apply sun cream, particularly on their face, use a big makeup brush. Obviously, you'll want to use an old one (or a cheap new one) but not only do the kids find it more fun, it's also easier to make sure all those niggly bits are covered.

I always aim to put their sun cream on before we get to the beach. Once we're there, all they want to do is play and compliance is everything when it comes to kids and sunscreen application!

BTW, I also now apply fake tan to my face like this, so no more orange hands.

Keeping Valuables Safe

While you're at the beach, it's obviously not a good idea to leave your valuables unattended. But if I've ever needed to, I hide them inside a nappy and seal that up inside a nappy bag. Hopefully, if anyone comes looking for valuables, that's the last thing they'd think to take away with them! You can also buy fake empty sun cream storage to put your valuables in, too.

Protect Your Phone

Before you spend lots of money on a fancy phone case to protect your mobile from sand and water, a freezer bag works just as well. Put your phone in the bag and seal it up! Your phone will still work and you can even take pictures as normal.

High Visibility

On holiday I like to dress my boys in bright swimwear and T-shirts. That way, I can easily spot them because the coloured clothing stands out. Great for busy theme parks as well.

Sand-Free Play Area

Bring a fitted sheet with you and spread it out on the sand facing upwards. Place heavier items like bags or shoes inside the scrunchy corners as anchors and pull the corners up over those items. This will create a nice little area with raised sides which doesn't get sandy. Ideal for your baby to sit and play in and for you to keep essentials away from the sand.

Beach Baby Seat

You can make a really sweet baby seat by digging a small hole and building up a bit of sand at the back to stop your little one falling backwards. Cover it with a blanket or towel and pop your baby in! A perfect place for them to sit and play safely.

Happy Nappies

Did you know that you can reuse swim nappies? If your baby hasn't spent long in the water and the nappy comes out clean, you can rinse it out, let it dry in the sun and use again. This is such a great hack, as they sometimes only get used for five minutes and they're not cheap or eco-friendly to keep replacing.

Don't Forget . . .

These essential items should be in your beach bag no matter what.

RUBBISH BAG

Remember to pack a large spare empty bag for all your rubbish (folded into a triangle as explained on page 51) as you're unlikely to be sat within arm's reach of a bin and this will help keep your area tidy. If there are recycling bins at the beach, you can separate it all out as you're leaving, otherwise, take it home with you and sort into the recycling there.

WET BAG

A waterproof or canvas bag is needed for transporting wet swimming costumes and trunks back at the end of the day.

CHANGE OF CLOTHES

The law of the beach dictates that at least one of your gang is going to manage to soak themselves from head to toe while fully clothed. Roll a change of clothes per child into separate bundles and put them into individual freezer bags.

KNIT WITS

Even when it's sunny, it can still feel quite chilly at the beach, especially if you're in the UK. The kids keep warm by running around and wrapping themselves up in a towel so pack a fine-knit cardi or sweater for yourself in case the wind whips up.

Bottles of Frozen Water

The day before you go to the beach, pop a couple of big plastic bottles of water in the freezer. These will help keep any picnic food fresh and chilled as well as providing much-needed ice cold drinks of water as they melt in the sun. You can do this with the kids' juice cartons, too.

Portable Potty

If you're toilet training your toddler, a portable potty could come in very handy at the beach for number twos when you might be a fair walk away from the public loos. Because when they gotta go . . . Alternatively, designate a spare bucket.

Handwashing Bucket

As soon as you arrive at the beach, fill a bucket with water and put it to one side. Before anyone dips sandy hands into the picnic bag, they have to wash them off in there. Them's the rules! No one likes a gritty sandwich.

Keep It Cool

A squirty bottle of fresh water, kept cold by storing it with your bigger frozen bottles, is a lovely way to cool down hot and bothered faces and relieve eyes which are stinging from the salt water.

Making a Mesh

We love to take two large mesh bags on holiday for laundry (one for colours, one for lights), but they're also great for the beach. Pack up your buckets, spades and any other paraphernalia into one of these and much of the sand will drop out through the mesh with a few shakes. Most of the rest will fall out as you depart so you're not bringing half the beach back home with you.

GAME-CHANGING GADGET ALERT

Pop-Up Tent

These are a genius way to keep little ones in the shade. They fold down so compactly and weigh next to nothing, so it's no bother to add them into the mix.

Spare Water Bottle

If you've got room, keep aside one full bottle of water for when you get back to the car or leave the beach to wash the last stubborn bits of sand from hands and feet.

Pre-Fasten the Seatbelts

Returning to the car on a swelteringly hot day means the whole interior is scorching and anything metallic like the seatbelt buckles can scold the skin. Ouch! Clipping the seatbelts into the buckle before you leave the car for the day means they won't heat up and cause you all to yelp in pain later on. You can also rotate the steering wheel so it's upside down and won't burn the driver's hands on the return home.

Mark Your Territory

Use a brightly-coloured spinner windmill as a landmark – if older children are running off and enjoying the freedom of the beach, they need to find their way back again. And even just a few minutes of being lost on a beach is heart-in-mouth time for parents and children.

Moment for you

Smoothie Operator

When your energy levels need a boost, a delicious and nutritious smoothie can often do the trick. Here's a quick and easy recipe which will put a pep in your step!

Serves 1

INGREDIENTS
- ½ avocado
- handful of spinach
- handful of kale
- 50g pineapple chunks
- 300ml coconut water, or oat or unsweetened almond milk
- dash of chopped ginger

Add all the ingredients to a blender and whizz together until smooth. Serve chilled.

Final Word: Sunny days at the beach are gorgeous but, with children, they can also be exhausting. Hopefully all of these hacks combined will help you keep your cool and allow you to have some relaxation time – and make sure you keep some aftersun in the fridge for you to soothe your tired limbs and skin at the end of the day.

Chapter 15

Getaway Godsends

Amid the bikinis, trunks, T-shirts and shorts, I have an array of other items which I now couldn't leave for our holidays without. I'm not saying they will make or break your holiday, but whether you're jetting off to a sunny resort, heading to a country cottage or braving it with a camping trip, there's plenty here to help you while you're there.

YOU MAY NEED:

- Multi-socket extension lead
- Head torch
- Parcel tape
- Tumble dryer sheets
- Petroleum jelly
- Drinking straws
- Pill box

Matt's Travel Adaptor Hack

My husband claims to have invented this one! And credit where it's due, I'll let him have it . . . We all take so many electrical items on holiday these days with phones, headphones and tablets that need charging, but rather than buying lots of travel adaptors, just pack one, along with a multiple socket. Pretty clever, eh?!

DIY Blackout Blind

Sometimes you arrive at your holiday destination only to find that the blinds or curtains in your little one's room aren't enough to block out the early morning sunlight. You can buy travel blackout blinds with suction cups to stick to the window, but a cheap and effective hack is to pack some tin foil and tape in your suitcase and fix the foil to the windows to act as a blackout. It might not be the prettiest window dressing, but it will allow your baby (and your older ones, too!) to sleep and that's the main thing!

Hair Band Brilliance

Use hair bands to stop all your chargers and cables becoming entangled. Spiral the cable around your fingers to make a loop and then tie the band in the middle so it's cinched in like a figure eight.

Swimwear Solution

If your return flight, train or ferry isn't until later in the day and you have use of a pool until then, your kids will probably want to use that time to be in the water. Pack a wet bag to contain all of their swimming items and then seal it up so it doesn't make everything else in your suitcase damp on the way home.

Hanging Bags

If there's a shortage of surface space at your hotel room or apartment, a toiletry bag with a hook means you can hang everything up out of the way when you're not using it.

Light Headed

If you're sharing a room or tent with the kids while on holiday, a head torch is very useful if you want to read your book at night without waking them up with the main light or bedside lamp.

Got It Taped

If you're going on a self-catering holiday, a roll of parcel tape strategically applied to cupboards and wardrobe doors will prevent your baby or toddler from getting into every exciting nook and cranny.

Staying Fresh

I like to pack a box of tumble dryer sheets as they have so many uses when travelling. A couple in your dirty laundry bag means you're not coming home to a fortnight's build-up of musty-smelling clothes to wash. Popping a couple into the hotel or apartment drawers when you arrive will help your clothes keep smelling fresh and they're also very good at removing deodorant marks from your favourite holiday 'little black dress'.

If you're camping, putting a sheet inside each sleeping bag at the end of the trip will make sure everything smells hunky-dory when you come to use the bags again.

Testing the Temperature

Whether it's down to the change in climate, the food, the proximity to so many other people, the tiredness or the over-excitement, kids often get sick on holiday. I always take a little digital thermometer so if they do become poorly, we can monitor their temperature.

Keep It Clean

Washing clothes in a sink is not many people's vision of a relaxing holiday, but if you can do a couple of half loads while you're there, it means you won't have to lug quite as many clothes with you and it will reduce the work when you're back. Pasta sauce, olive oil and makeup are all best removed as early as possible rather than waiting until you get home.

You can pick up bottles of travel wash, but one teaspoon of shampoo in a sink of hot water (use cold if the items are delicate) does the job. Stir the water so the shampoo forms suds and then leave the clothes to soak for 10 minutes. Massage the most soiled areas, rinse through with non-soapy water, gently wring out and then air dry.

Marvellous Muslins

Not just good for mopping up all manner of baby mess, muslins also make excellent emergency sun hats with a few well-positioned knots. And, when damp with cold water, they are lovely to cool down with while placed on the forehead or draped around the back of the neck. So wonderfully multi-functional!

Other uses include:

- The perfect breastfeeding cover (I used to shove it under my bra strap and drape it over me)
- Wiping up spills
- Swaddle for newborns or a lightweight breathable blanket.
- Changing mat sheet to take away the coldness of the mat
- Car window shade
- Comforter

GAME-CHANGING GADGET ALERT

Sand-Repellent Beach Towel

You can get very clever towels which are sand-resistant, dry you quickly and are made of a microfibre material so they roll up really compact in your case. They are also incredibly lightweight.

Back-Up Clothes

You never know what accident or spillage might be just around the corner, so I prepare a little bundle of back-up clothes for each child, which I carry in my hand luggage. There's always one, isn't there? Sports kits are best as they're so lightweight.

Petroleum Jelly

It's hard to think of a product which is as versatile as petroleum jelly and a mini pot of it goes a long way while taking up no room in your luggage at all. My favourite uses for it are:

- Eye makeup remover
- Lip balm
- Removing rings from fingers swollen with the heat
- Taming eyebrows
- Preventing chafing
- Healing small cuts
- Shining shoes
- Putting around your nails to prevent varnish getting on to fingers
- Adding a little holiday dewiness to your cheeks

Luck of the Straw

I use drinking straws to store my necklaces while travelling as it stops them getting all tangled en route. Cut them down a little, feed the necklace through and then fasten it. Take spares for the journey home. Also, a pill box is great for storing rings and earrings.

Seal the Deal

Take a mini roll of tape in your toiletries bag – I use this to seal the tops of all my cosmetic bottles on the way there and back. An explosion of moisturiser and hair conditioner is not what you want to be dealing with at either end of the holiday.

Portable Charger

A necessary addition to your holiday items, especially if you enjoy venturing out and about and will be relying on the map on your phone. Just make sure you've charged it before you leave for the day!

Eat Breakfast

This sounds so simple but as mums we often forget about ourselves because we're so busy worrying about what our kids are eating and getting them ready for the day. Resolve to treat yourself with the same love and care as you do your kids and start the day with a healthy breakfast, like porridge with fruit. Or indulge in pancakes or crumpets with jam.

You could even suggest that your gang (with some supervision) serve you breakfast in bed one Sunday morning. They will enjoy the task and you will get a lie-in plus something yummy.

Final Word: *My travel videos on YouTube are always the most popular – it seems we're all looking for ways to take the pressure off family holidays. I could dish out practical tips until the cows come home, but my best advice would be to remember that, a bit like Christmas, the 'perfect' holiday probably doesn't exist. At various points, something (or things) will go wrong, kids will become tired and ratty and the weather won't play ball. Let it go. You are there with your gang and that's all that matters.*

Habits

Chapter 16

Pack Like a Pro

Packing for the whole family to cover for every eventuality and potential weather scenario takes an awful lot of thought. I often struggle to know where to start and the overwhelm is wearing. This chapter will look at ways to tackle the task of packing efficiently and how to make sure you don't forget anything and stop your suitcase contents resembling a jumble sale by the time you arrive at your destination.

YOU MAY NEED:
- Packing cubes
- Shower caps
- Mini reusable containers
- Handheld spring scales

List Assists

You know me, lists give me life! You can save a general packing list on your laptop or phone and adapt it holiday by holiday as a lot of the items will cross over, so you'll need them regardless of where you're going. Keep essentials at the top and then jot down everything else for each person in the family. It's also worth making a list of smaller items that you need to pack at the very last minute on the morning of the day you travel to be sure that you don't forget anything.

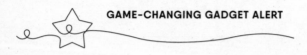

GAME-CHANGING GADGET ALERT

Packing Cubes

These things have changed my life. I bought a pack a few years ago and they are brilliant for grouping items together in your suitcase, especially smaller baby clothes, or things like your swimming costumes or dresses. It keeps everything organised and makes unpacking at the end of your journey a doddle.

Roll With It

Rolling rather than folding helps everything stay crease-free. The last thing you want to be doing on holiday is reaching for the iron and this technique is a much more compact way of packing, so it also allows you to squeeze a few extra items into your case.

Shower Caps for Shoes

Save a stash of hotel shower caps or blue shoe covers from the kids' swimming lessons and fit them on your shoes before packing them to avoid getting dirt on your clean clothes or making the inside of your case grubby. They're great for muddy pram wheels if you want to protect the boot of your car, as well.

Also, pack socks inside your shoes for an instant space-saver and a way to help shoes keep their shape during the journey.

Decant Beauty Products

Miniature versions of toiletry products are cute, but they're more expensive and obviously not great for the environment. Decant your favourite products into reusable containers so that you can travel with everything you need. You can get these really cheaply on your local high street, but even better if you can repurpose old ones. Wash them out once empty and use again and again.

Transporting Sun Hats

As well as looking chic, a wide-brimmed straw hat is a must for me to keep the sun off my face. But they get squashed to within an inch of their lives inside suitcases! Avoid this happening by packing the head of the hat with clothes or packing cubes and it will keep its shape.

Weight Check

Weighing your cases before you leave with a handheld set of spring scales will mean you don't end up having to swap clothes between bags at check-in when one of them exceeds the allowance. Yep, I've been that person.

Make Your Luggage Stand Out

Attaching a bright piece of ribbon or a colourful tag to the handle of your suitcases will make them instantly recognisable. And adding 'fragile' tape to it might – might – mean baggage staff handle it with extra care.

Be Ruthless With Your Shoes

I love shoes as much as the next woman, but it's just not practical or necessary to take several pairs away with you on holiday. I used to pack six or seven pairs, but for a beach holiday I've learned that you really only need one pair of heels or evening shoes (I take a gold or nude pair), one pair of flip flops or sliders and I'll wear trainers to travel in.

The kids only need a smart pair of sandals for the evening, waterproof shoes for the poolside or beach and trainers for travelling in and playing football once we're there.

Bag Up Kids' Outfits

This won't be for everyone as it does take quite a bit of pre-holiday planning. But for those of you who like to be super duper organised, within my packing cubes I love using large freezer bags to contain each daily outfit for the boys, which reduces time spent deciding on what to wear and increases independence in everyday dressing skills for little ones. I also do this when the boys go on overnight school trips or off to camp. I put an outfit in each bag and tell them to put the used and dirty clothes back in the bags. Not that they ever do that . . .

Here's a suggested children's packing list for a beach holiday. You might want to add to it or tweak it to reduce the load, but I hope it serves at least as a starting point:

- 2 outfits to travel in (there and back)
- 1 cardigan, hoodie or lightweight jacket in case it's cold
- 1 outfit per day plus 3 extra lightweight options (football kits or dresses)
- 1 evening outfit per day if you like to get dressed up at night (T-shirts and shorts might be able to be re-worn the next day)
- 2 swimwear (they can wear one while the other dries)
- 1 pair of pyjamas for every few days
- 1 pair of trainers (worn to travel)
- 1 pair of sliders or sandals
- 1 pair of smart sandals or shoes for evening
- 1 pair of underwear per day plus 3 extras
- 1 pair of socks per day
- 1 sunhat and sunglasses

Limit Your Makeup

When I'm travelling I really try to limit the number of beauty products I take. On one trip I forgot all of it, but that's another story! You really don't need much and I've also learned that trying anything new probably isn't the best idea. Oldies but goodies only! I take one each of:

- Concealer
- Lightweight foundation with SPF
- Bronzer
- Blusher
- Eyebrow gel
- Waterproof mascara
- Lipstick

Keep Toiletries to a Minimum

Check ahead to see if the accommodation you're staying at provides basic toiletries as this will save you lugging any over from home. I also like to use a two-in-one shampoo and conditioner for the kids (just one container required) and you can buy toothpaste tablets which are eco-friendly, mess-free and save space rather than taking an entire tube.

Car Seat Trick

If you're hiring a car at your destination and taking your own child's car seat, put it in a zip-up bag for check in. Because this does not count as part of your baggage allowance, you can fill the bag with extra nappies, wipes and other baby bits and bobs at no extra cost which will free up space in your luggage.

What a Carry On

Getting the contents of the hand luggage right can make or break a journey with kids! I keep a fail-safe list of must-pack items to ensure our travels are as peaceful as possible. Here's what works for us:

- Tablets and headphones
- Little toy – mine love blind bag surprises
- Colouring or activity book with marker pens or crayons
- An age-appropriate book each
- Snacks such as fruit, breadsticks, fruit pouches, dry cereal
- Treats for desperate times and to help their ears during the descent
- Empty kids' cups that you can fill on board
- Wipes
- Nappies if needed
- Spare top and cardigan
- Milk if needed for a baby – you can also order and collect this at some airport terminals
- Medicine – teething products if needed and pain relief just in case

Moment for you

Meet a Friend

Often our children seem to have better social lives than we do! But it's so important to nurture your own friendships and so if you can, arrange to meet a friend for a kid-free catch-up over coffee, an exercise class or a walk in the park. If it's hard to get out, schedule a video call and have a virtual catch up. Keep those connections.

Final Word: *I've actually grown to love packing over the years. I like being methodical and a neatly packed suitcase with everything in order is one of life's pleasures as far as I'm concerned! What I don't enjoy quite so much is the unpacking. There's no clearer sign that the holiday is O.V.E.R. and that can feel disheartening and demotivating.*

But I'm a big believer in treating it like a plaster and ripping it off, getting everything done as soon as possible, even if that means within minutes of walking back through the door. You'll feel a million times better than if you leave suitcases to fester!

Chapter 17

Getting Ahead of Going Away

Holidays should be an opportunity to switch off from the daily grind and spend quality time with the people you love the most. We've always prioritised going away as a family because we find we really connect when there are none of the usual distractions of being at home. It doesn't have to be to a fancy resort – it's more about the change of scene – a camping weekend, a country cottage or a few staycation days at the Great British seaside (take a brolly!) will do the job just as well.

In this final chapter on travel, I'm going to whiz you through some tricks of the trade which will ensure your time away and your return home are as relaxing as possible.

Stick to the List

Make a comprehensive list of everything you need to buy and stick to it. It's very easy to get to the shops pre-holiday and be swayed by items you don't really need (I'm guilty as charged!). This also means you don't forget anything and end up having to buy an emergency supply, which eats into your holiday spending budget.

Shop Around for Insurance

Use comparison sites for the best deals and buy your insurance as soon as you book your holiday to cover cancellation or illness. You can find comparison websites online to check which deal is best for you. It's also worth finding out if you're already covered through your bank account – lots of people are but don't always realise.

Travel at Night

If going by car, choose the time of your journey carefully. We've found that travelling at bedtime tends to be easiest. Get the kids all ready for bed (fed, bathed and in their PJs), bundle them into the car with their travel pillows and blankets and then transfer them straight to their beds when you get to your destination. When it works and you've got all of them simultaneously sleeping in the back, it's cloud nine territory!

Keep Emergency Items in the Car

I keep a stash of essentials in the car at all times, which makes even short journeys easier. In the boot I have a large towel which is great for impromptu picnics or if one of the kids decides to jump in a fountain when we're out. I keep one change of outfit just in case – as we have three boys, I pack a set of my middle son's clothes which would fit any one of them in an emergency. When we were still using nappies, I also had a nappy changing kit with spare nappies, wipes, barrier cream and hand sanitiser.

Clean the House

Again, this is about being kind to your future self. Before you leave for your holiday, give the house a once over with the vacuum cleaner, make the beds, clear surfaces, put stray shoes away, don't leave dirty dishes in the sink and empty the bins. Make sure everyone in your household pitches in with this.

Coming home to a clean and tidy house after a week or two away will feel blissful and allow you to unpack and get the washing on without feeling hindered by your other To-Do list.

Family and Friends Railcard

If you're travelling anywhere by train, one of these will save you so much money on your tickets. It costs just £30 and as long as you're travelling with at least one child, it gives you one third off adult tickets and 60 per cent off children's tickets throughout Great Britain for a whole year. One card can be used for up to four adults and four children travelling together and even taking into account that initial £30 fee, you'll be saving money from the very first journey.

Timely Airport Arrivals

We always aim to get to the airport a full three hours before the flight. It's so much better to be able to get through security without a panic and then to have time for a coffee and a bite to eat in departures. I also like to mooch around the duty free and to sample some of the perfumes. Lots of airports have soft play areas for children to run about in, which is great to give them a bit of a stretch before they get on the plane.

Orderly Laundry

When we go away, I take two thin mesh laundry bags – one for lights and one for darks. This makes laundry so much easier when you arrive home and need to sort through your many, many loads.

Scan Important Documents

If the worst happens and you mislay your phone or purse or have them stolen, then having copies of your passport, driving licence, travel documents and anything else important scanned and emailed to yourself means you'll still have access to all of these by logging into your account from another device. Hopefully you won't need it, but if you do, it will make the process a little less painful.

Neighbourhood Watch

Everybody needs good neighbours . . . Remember to ask them to put your bins out and make sure any mail is pushed through the letterbox so it doesn't advertise you're away.

Passport Panic

A quick reminder that kids' passports only run for five years and if any of you are travelling within six months of expiry, the passport is not valid. I know so many people are caught out by that little quirk in the system. Set alarms on your phone for 12 months before they expire so you get it sorted in good time.

Making Memories

Bring a scrapbook and encourage older children to keep a journal of the holiday while you're there. They might want to save shells from the beach, a cocktail umbrella from the bar, a train ticket or buy a postcard of the place you're staying. Print out photos when you're home and they can add those in too.

Stock the Fridge

Put a loaf of bread and some milk in the freezer for when you return (milk can be defrosted quickly in warm water) and make sure there are a few snacks for the kids – ice pops ready if they need a refreshment after the long journey back to base.

I also like to do an online shop on the last day of the holiday and schedule it for delivery at a time you know all the unpacking will have been done and the first load of washing completed so those tasks don't end up clashing.

Moment for you

Focus on the Positive

Every evening I like to think about what was the best thing that happened that day and write down three things I'm grateful for. We've also got in the habit of asking the boys to think about that too. Some days are harder than others, but we all have things to be thankful for, so I try to find something, no matter how small and it always helps to end the day on a positive note.

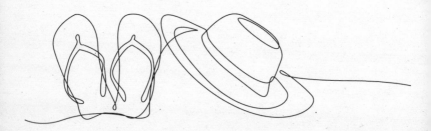

𝔉inal 𝔚ord: *It almost defeats the purpose of a holiday if you're starting it off uptight and in a state of high stress from having been running around like a headless chicken until the last second. Who wants to begin a holiday feeling more frazzled than ever?*

It comes back to the philosophy we've spoken a lot about in this book around being kind to your future self. When you get everything done in good time, you can head off on holiday with a clear head as soon as you lock the front door behind you. You deserve that.

IV:

School
Rules

The start of a new school year is always exciting, for us parents as well as the kids! But with so much to plan, dates to remember and uniforms to organise, things can quickly unravel unless you have a few good routines to hold it all in place.

In this section I'll be sharing my top hacks for everything to do with school, from the handy portable homework station to the assembly line lunches, which are a clever way of getting your children involved in making their own nutrition-packed meals. And there are no shortage of time-saving tips which will help you navigate the daily dash to arrive at the school gates on schedule and with your sanity intact.

Hacks

Chapter 18

Hassle-Free Homework

There aren't many kids who enjoy being dragged away from a pressing engagement with a games console or their favourite TV show in order to do their homework. I know this is a common battleground for families and we are no different.

I have a stockpile of hacks and flexible rules for getting the homework done and handed in on time without the whole thing descending into conflict. We're not perfect and there are some days when we end up locking horns, but generally things run according to plan if we use the following tips and tricks.

YOU MAY NEED:
- Noice-cancelling headphones
- Accordian file
- Tiered tray

Portable Homework Station

If your child doesn't have a desk, a portable homework station is a good alternative. I picked up a caddy with a handle from a pound store and filled it with all the necessary homework bits and bobs; scissors, glue, ruler, pens, pencils, etc. The kids can take their portable station with them wherever they're going to do homework and everything they need is in one place – which also means no excuses!

Dedicate a Space

Wherever your child is doing their homework, make a clear, comfortable space for them to sit down and do it. If it's the kitchen table, remove any clutter beforehand and allow them to feel that this is their designated little area, even if only for the next 20 minutes. If they're doing homework in their room make sure they keep their desk area tidy and don't allow it to become over-run with football cards, comics or piles of books. A tidy desk equals a tidy mind.

Turn off the Tech

Homework is best done with no distractions even in the background, so make it a tech-free zone by completely switching off the consoles and TV (rather than just pausing them) and taking away your child's mobile phone if they have one. I even set my own phone to Do Not Disturb mode so the whole vibe is peaceful and without any interruptions.

Block Out the Noise

Toddlers and babies tend not to comply with the 'quiet, please' requests and if your older children are doing their homework in a communal space then that can be difficult. A pair of noise-cancelling headphones while they're working can work well in this situation.

Brain Food

A bowl of healthy snacks such as nuts or chopped fruit as well as a cup of water will provide fuel for hardworking minds and stop requests for food and drinks being used as cunning delay tactics. I arrange five different snacks on a plate – grapes, cucumber, carrot sticks, nuts and some crackers, for instance – and my kids love the surprise element about what they're going to get.

All in Good Time

For the longer, more intensive homework sessions, a timer can help maintain focus as well as allowing regular breaks to work towards. Depending on the age of your child, set a timer for between 10–20 minutes with a bleeper scheduled for a 5-minute break at the end of that stint. We have a timer cube which I found online – it's so cute and really helps avoid the temptation to procrastinate.

Breath of Fresh Air

Open windows to keep fresh, cool air circulating, which will help them stay alert while working. And encourage them to go out-side during breaks for a walk around the block or a kickabout in the garden. That way they won't go into a slump and find it difficult to get back to work afterwards.

Make It Fun

Older children will want to get on with their homework alone, but making things a bit fun for your littler people can go a long way towards keeping them engaged. We've used cereal pieces for fraction work which they get to eat afterwards. For trickier spellings we'll make up a silly song to help them remember it easily. Here are a few good hacks to help remember the most notoriously tricky words:

BELIEVE – Never believe a LIE (to remember it's L-I-E in the middle)

RHYTHM – Rhythm Helps Your Two Hips Move

BECAUSE – Big Elephants Can Always Understand Small Elephants

NECESSARY – One Collar, two Sleeves (one C, two Ss)

STATIONERY – E for Envelope (to remember this spelling refers to paper goods)

STATIONARY – A for Anchored (to remember this spelling refers to standing still)

Head Over Heels

This might sound a little weird but a few handstands mid-homework session can really help maintain concentration levels. The inverted position increases blood flow to the brain, which aids mental focus, plus the kids have fun getting up there! Get them to do this up against a wall – you may need to help pull their legs up for the first few attempts.

Colour Coded Clock

This is a great way to get your kids to follow a morning or afternoon routine while also teaching them to tell the time. Colour in sections of your clock using a dry erase marker and label them accordingly. If you get home at 4pm, then 4–5pm might be homework time with 5–6pm play time. The kids can look at the clock and know what's coming up.

Storing Work

Kids bring an awful lot of stuff home from school and pre-school. As much as the sentimental side of us would love to keep everything, it's just not practical. I don't always have time to sort through it on the go, so I have an expandable accordion file for each child and over the course of the year, any piece of work they bring home goes in there. At the end of the summer term, I set aside some time to go through each of them and decide which to chuck and which to keep for their memory boxes.

Photographic Evidence

If you're short on storage or wall space, take photos of each piece of work rather than keeping the item itself. You can create a file for these digital pictures which will last forever and you could even make a photo book for each year, which is a lovely keepsake to look back on as they get older.

Scheduling Homework

If there's homework set, get your child into the routine of doing it at an agreed time – ideally not last thing on a Sunday evening! We generally aim to get it done as soon as they arrive home as I find if we leave it any later, the kids are too tired to focus. There's also the incentive to get it out of the way so they can enjoy the rest of their evening.

Pencil Grip

If your child is struggling to hold a pencil in the tripod grip, try this. With the pencil pointing towards your child, ask them to pinch the nib end of it with their thumb, middle and index fingers. Then get them to flip the top of the pencil towards themselves so that it rests in their hand, while still being pinched between the thumb and fingers.

Filing System

If you have more than one child, keeping track of all the homework books and worksheets can prove a challenge! Giving each child a different coloured document folder for them to keep anything to do with homework in will help stop any loose worksheets going astray.

If you have space, a tiered tray with one shelf designated per child can be used to house completed homework before it's handed in.

Moment for you

Charity Shop Rummage

There's nothing quite like finding a gem of a bargain at a charity shop. And the rummage that leads to that discovery is half the fun.

After your next declutter or clothes cull, take a bag of donations to your local charity shop and enjoy a good browse while you're there. If there are a few on the same high street, turn it into a charity shop crawl – a bit like a pub crawl but way more wholesome!

Final Word: *Kids need downtime and there will be some days there's no point in coming down heavy on the homework front. Do what you can to reduce distractions and stress, to make it more fun and to remain supportive and calm. Don't let it descend into a power struggle.*

Chapter 19

Smashing the School Run

By the time I've dropped off the kids in the morning, I feel like I've run a marathon. In a way, I kind of have! Even if you've prepped as much as you can the night before, there's still a huge amount to do in the mornings to ensure everyone is washed, fed, dressed and out of the door on time.

The next few pages will help your morning routine become a well-oiled machine – this is how to make the school run a walk in the park.

YOU MAY NEED:
- Toothbrushing timer
- Foot measurer

Sound the Alarm

If you're prone to running late in the morning, set a load of alarm reminders on your phone. They might be things like 'don't forget the school bags' or 'has everyone brushed their teeth?' and it can be really useful to have these little prompts. I live a lot of my daily life by various alerts on my phone and have an alarm that goes off at the end of each school day to remind me to wrap up whatever I'm doing and get ready for school pick-up.

Moment of Tooth

Encourage your children to brush their teeth with a toothbrushing timer – there are loads of great two-minute timers on YouTube. If you choose one with a character they love, it can really help having that to guide them when they're little.

Personal Pegs

Give each child their own peg which is where their coat and bag are kept when not in use. This harks back to the 'one touch method' I talked about on page 72 – the kids come through the door and hang their outerwear up in one direct movement. No more coats on the floor or searching the house high and low in the morning for a school bag which has gone walkabout. They can personalise their pegs with a sticker they've designed themselves which will get their creative juices flowing and encourage them to take ownership of the peg itself – making them more likely to use it!

Right Foot Forward

Once kids are old enough to dress themselves, it does save a lot of time in the mornings. But I can't be the only parent to have realised when we've arrived at school that their child has banana feet because their shoes are on the wrong way round. If you get a sticker (this works best if it's an easily recognisable image, like a train or an elephant), cut in half and put one half inside the left shoe and the other half inside the right shoe, they just have to put the shoes side by side to see the complete picture and know which way round to wear them. In the past I've also used a permanent marker pen for this and drawn half a heart or a half a smiley face on each shoe.

GAME-CHANGING GADGET ALERT

Measuring Feet

Speaking of shoes, my kids all hated going to have their feet measured so when I found you could buy foot measurers to use at home, I did a little air punch. I'd totally recommend getting one if you can because it saves having to cart them all to the shops for new shoes – I measure at home and then order online.

Tying Ties

If your school uniform includes a tie, 'fake it till you make it' and stick to the elasticated versions while they're young. When your children get a bit older and they want or need to tie it themselves, show them the four steps to remember:

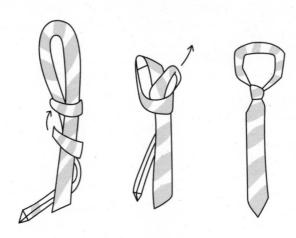

1. Place the tie around your neck with the wider end on your right side and a bit lower down than the thinner end.
2. Cross the wide end under the thinner end and then over it again so it's heading back towards the right hand side.
3. Take the wide end up through the neck loop in the middle.
4. Pull your tie through the knot you've created and adjust.

These steps can be condensed into an easy-to-remember rhyme:

> *Wide under thin,*
> *And then over again,*
> *Wide up the middle*
> *And then through with a wiggle.*

Shoelace Shenanigans

For an easy life, I'm a big advocate of keeping kids in Velcro-fastening trainers for as long as possible! But there will come a time when your kids do need to tie their own shoelaces and a great way to teach them is to use the very simple Bunny Ears (or two loop) method:

1. Cross both ends of the lace then tuck the top one under and through the hole. Pull both ends to tighten.
2. Make a loop with one lace and pinch the end tightly.
3. Make another loop with the other lace and pinch – now you have your two bunny ears.
4. Keep pinching both bunny ears as you cross one over the other.

5. Bring the bottom bunny ear around and feed it through the hole you've created.
6. Pull both ears to tighten.

This will take a bit of time and patience to master, but it's really good for their fine motor skills and once they've got it, they don't forget it.

There's also a little rhyme they can chant while they're trying, to help keep them on track:

> *Bunny ears, bunny ears, playing by a tree*
> *Criss-crossed the tree, trying to catch me*
> *Bunny ears, bunny ears, jumped into the hole,*
> *Popped out the other side, beautiful and bold.*

Coats on Quick

A quick and easy way for smaller kids to put their coat on without getting into a tangle is for them to lay it on the floor with the inside of the jacket facing up. Standing at the hood/collar end, they place their arms through the sleeves, bring the coat up and then flip the whole thing up and over their head. They can normally be taught to do this from about the age of two and it looks so cool and effortless!

Uniforms on Last

Don't even think about putting uniforms on before breakfast or teeth brushing because we all know how that story ends. Uniforms go on last when all the potential for slops and dribbles is out of the way.

Hair Straightener Hack

If you like your kids to look pristine for school, a pair of hair straighteners can tackle shirt creases in seconds and save you having to dig out the iron when the clock says you should be halfway out the front door.

Hair Band Storage

All my boys have short hair, so this isn't one I've ever needed. But my friends with long-haired boys and girls tell me that the morning search for a spare hair tie can add several minutes you don't have. Keeping hair bands looped around a shower curtain ring is a great solution here. Once they're on there, they don't go missing and you can clearly see when you're running low and need to do a sweep of the house to find the ones that got away.

Wiped Out

Keep a face cloth handy by the door for the milk moustaches, toothpaste lips and runny noses that need a last-minute swipe before you leave for the day. We also have a second set of toothbrushes and toothpaste in the downstairs loo, which saves them having to run back upstairs if they've somehow managed to dodge that task until we're nearly out the door.

Winter Warmers

There's always more stuff to find room for in the winter thanks to all the layers we need to keep vaguely warm! We've got a basket for each of us for hats, scarves and gloves, which makes it easy to grab and go as well as chuck items back in again when we get home.

I'm also a big fan of a hanging shoe rack which can go over the back of an under stairs cupboard door if you have one. You can use the compartments to store everyone's winter accessories so they're not causing clutter in the hallway.

Get Ready Box

Keep one of these in the kitchen or living room and use it to hold hairbrushes, toothbrushes, hair gel, hair bands, spare socks, sunscreen – anything you might need quickly as you're leaving the house. Use strips of cardboard to create dividers so that items don't get jumbled up.

Daily Checklist

Having a chart pinned somewhere very visible with an itemised checklist for each day is really helpful. You can give it a quick glance before you leave to make sure you've not forgotten anything. For example, depending on your children's schedules, Monday might have reading books and football kit listed, Tuesday might have violin and spellings . . . and so on. In the summer I add sunscreen to each day so I don't forget to put it on them.

Two-Minute Makeup

Somewhere amid getting everyone else organised, I have to make myself look semi-presentable! I've managed to get my school morning makeup routine down to a finely-tuned two-minute operation, which goes something like this:

1. Tinted moisturiser applied with my hands
2. Concealer
3. A tiny bit of blush to make me look alive!

I have fake eyelashes applied every few weeks and my eyebrows are microbladed – not having to worry about lashes or brows in the morning saves me so much time.

Two-For-One Coffee

Here's a thing – make two coffees in the morning, one to drink straight away and one to stick in a vacuum-insulated flask or cup to take on the school run with you or to have when you get back home or arrive at work.

Moment for you

Journaling

If you find it hard to go to sleep at night – perhaps you've got lots of things going round your brain – put pen to paper and get those thoughts out of your head. It might be tasks you need to do tomorrow, or something that's worrying you or what you've been up to.

It could be an inspirational quote you've come across, a list of things you're feeling grateful for, general reflections on life or something funny the kids have said that day. Whatever it is, get it written down and it should bring you a sense of calm.

I always find it easier to get started if I've got some gorgeous stationery, so treat yourself to a lovely notebook, keep it on your bedside table and allocate some time each day – even a few minutes – so it becomes a ritual. Your journal can be whatever you want it to be.

𝓕inal 𝓦ord: *When I think of everything we have to manage before the clock strikes 9am, I honestly reckon we're all superhuman! It's not easy. Please know that I think you're a miracle worker. It's funny, isn't it? When the school run is a dim and distant memory, we'll probably look back on this time with huge affection and wish we could go back there, if only for a minute.*

Habits

Chapter 20

Fool-Proof Routines

In the last chapter we looked at the 'on the go' hacks you could introduce to make the mornings run smoother. I'm now going to talk about the longer-term practices – the habits – you can pick and choose to work into your life. They might take a little bit more planning, but it won't take long before they're embedded into the daily routine and making a big difference.

Get Everything Ready the Night Before

It sounds so obvious, but if you can get into the habit of sorting out everything you need for the morning the night before, it's a game-changer. Lay out the uniform (including socks and under-wear) so it's all ready to go, get the schoolbags and PE kits packed and line them up by the front door so by the time morning comes around, it's simply a case of grabbing and going. Older children can take responsibility for their own bags. I even lay out the cutlery, plates and bowls we'll need for breakfast because when you're trying to get everyone washed, dressed and out of the house in time for the school bell, every second counts!

Assembly Line Lunch Box

This one is probably for children aged eight and up but I love getting my kids to make their own packed lunches. Write out a checklist of everything they should include (sandwich, fruit, drink, treat, for example) and pop it inside their lunch box or bag. They can work their way through the list, making their own sandwich and finding the other items – we use a low shelf in the fridge for all lunch ingredients. It's another task that can be done the night before and will also build your child's confidence and independence. You can be around in a supervisory role and getting on with other chores while they toil away. But remember, supervisors require cups of tea!

Everything Uniform

Managing the supply and demand for school uniforms in our house keeps me constantly on my toes. And with sports clubs on different days of the week, there's a lot of washing to boss. Doing a load every morning, having looked ahead at who needs what for the next day is the only way to manage it all and stay one step ahead!

When it comes to organising it all, the over-the-door shoe storage systems I mentioned earlier are also brilliant for school uniform. Each child can have one for the inside of their wardrobe or the back of their bedroom door and you can use the individual compartments to store the uniform day by day. And I do love a multi-hanger for school trousers – you can hang up to four or five pairs on them and they take up so little space.

We also have an underwear system so I know which pants belong to which boy. One has solid colours, another has camo print and the third has characters or dinosaurs.

Wash Only What You Need

For environmental and time-saving reasons, I'm trying only to wash what absolutely needs it. After school I do a quick uniform check and if the blazers, jumpers, shorts and trousers look OK, I'll give them a quick spot clean with a cloth and put them out again for the next day.

Speaking of uniforms, here are a few ideas for keeping the expense down. Uniforms are so pricey and because little people grow so fast, the costs can mount up to become eye-watering so I hope some of the following can help make a difference.

- Lots of shops sell school trousers with a double hem. When your child is too tall for the trousers, just unpick the hem and iron out the crease for an extra few centimetres and possibly another six months' wear.
- If your school uniform is a standard colour, such as red, navy or green, it usually works out much cheaper to buy the sweaters, hoodies for PE and polo shirts at the supermarket and then find a local workwear or textiles shop to add the school badge to the items. Anecdotally, the supermarket

quality is often superior to the specialist suppliers with far less bobbling. Go, figure . . .

- Look out for uniform sales in shops and supermarkets. They're usually spread throughout the year but are rarely in the summer which is when there is most demand. If you can, size up and stock up for the following school year while the offers are on.
- Check out Facebook Marketplace or your local Freecycle site – there are usually people offloading second-hand uniforms which still have plenty of life left in them. And if there's not one organised already, speak to your school PTA about setting up a uniform swap or £1 sale.
- How many times have I found myself rifling through the school lost property box for lost sweaters? Too many. But I'd never have had a chance of reclaiming any of them if they weren't name tagged. We use customised stampers which add your child's name to the label of their clothes in seconds and last for about 50 washes. You can also get the iron on tags and a permanent marker pen works fine, too!

Five-Minute Warning

Put everyone on an alert five minutes before you're due to leave so the departure shouldn't come as a surprise to anyone. As the clock counts down, this time should be used for any last-minute toilet trips or drinks of water or putting shoes on. You could even turn it into a race as that can often get kids moving!

Prep Yourself

As well as putting out the kids' uniforms for the next day, I always take a couple of minutes to do the same for myself, too. Check the weather forecast, bear in mind what you're doing straight after the school run (heading to work, going to a meeting or an appointment, seeing a friend for a coffee, dragging yourself to the gym, popping to the supermarket) and plan your outfit accordingly. In the morning you can just throw it on without losing time rummaging for something suitable.

Reward Charts

I've always found these so motivating at any age – good work deserves praise and reward in all areas of life, including home-work! I like to give the kids a selection of rewards they can choose from to work towards across the week. Every bit of homework gets checked off with a star as they go and by Friday, if it's all been done then they can claim their reward which might be extra pocket money, some packs of football stickers or even a 'yes' day (although do make sure you think this one through . . .)

Contingency Minutes

Whatever your timetable for the morning routine is, build in some precious extra minutes to give yourself a bit of breathing space. Do this by starting a bit earlier than necessary or slightly over-estimating the time you'll need.

School Routine Chart

After a long summer break, the Easter holidays or a Christmas period of lazy mornings, a routine chart will help kids get back into the term time rhythm and habits. Our school routine chart simply lays out the tasks they need to get done in the morning before school, as well as the tasks they must do when they get home from school. Depending on their ages, your kids' morning and afternoon tasks might include:

AM
- Brush teeth
- Make beds
- Pack a snack
- Fill water bottle
- Check school bag is packed

PM
- Read for 15 minutes
- Do homework
- Lay out clothes for tomorrow
- Pack gear for any clubs tomorrow

Back to School Checklist

After the long summer holiday, there's always so much to organise and remember come 1 September. I have a saved checklist which I work my way through before the start of the new school year and it gets everything off on the right foot:

- Get a uniform checklist from the school and order as early as possible! Donate old clothes

- Do a full trial run of the uniform. Do we need a different size? Do trousers need to be taken up or let down?
- Check school shoes and buy next size up if needed
- Label EVERYTHING!
- If needed, buy a lunch box or bag and water bottle
- Do they need any stationery or a pencil case?
- Book haircuts (and if you're extra organised, dentist appointments so they won't have to miss time off school)
- Was there any homework they needed to complete during the summer?
- Pin up a school morning chart (I have a free printable on my website emilynorris.com if you're keen)
- Create a homework station (see page 203) or homework area
- Look at all the extra-curricular activities and work out your day-by-day schedule
- Stock up on healthy snacks and food for packed lunches.

And if you've got a child starting school this September (good luck, btw!), these extra checks might be helpful:

- Attend settling in visits (if your school has them) and talk about school throughout the summer. Things like: 'I wonder if Miss Smith likes the colour purple the same as you?'
- Get Velcro-fastening shoes for school shoes and use the sticker hack on page 210 so they place shoes on the right feet
- Can they dress themselves? If they struggle with an item such as socks, practise that in the lead-up to starting school
- Practise using a knife and fork if they're going to have school dinners
- Can they open their own storage containers or lunch box for snack and lunch times?

- Practise toileting. Are there any stages they struggle with such as pulling clothes down, wiping, flushing, pulling clothes up, washing hands?
- If your child is a keen learner, practise numbers and phonics either using flashcards or learning apps and read together
- Can they write their name or at least recognise it? Their name will be on coat hooks, and trays so it's really helpful if they can
- Is there a parents' WhatsApp group you can be added to or set up yourself? Could you do a meet-up before they start so they have some familiar faces on their first day?
- Practise the route to school
- Be positive! Children take their social cues from us, so if they see we're anxious or upset they may feel that way too. Try to be as happy and positive as possible until they're in the classroom (then have a good cry when you've gone round the corner!).

Moment for you

Go off Grid

Designate an hour in the evening, once the kids are all in bed, to switch off your phone and feel completely free of WhatsApp messages ping-ping-pinging, work emails and the endless scrolling we're all guilty of doing without even thinking. Use the time to read a book or meditate or simply close your eyes and enjoy the silence.

A morning routine for every household will vary depending on preferences and family dynamics. I get asked a lot about how our mornings work, so here's an example of what typically happens for us:

6am: Emily and Matt wake up
6.15am: We get dressed for the day
6.45am: Wake up the kids
7am: Prepare breakfast and eat together
7.30am: Kids (who can) make their beds, dishes washed
8am: Help children get dressed and ready for school
8.30am: Drop off children at school or walk them to the bus stop
8.45am: Get home and do a quick 10-minute tidy up of the kitchen
9am: Start work

When Your Child Is Unwell . . .

Sickness bugs are grim for everyone but especially so for kids and it's horrible to see them so poorly and lethargic. Here are my best tips for helping you through the worst of it:

- Washing hands is so important – 80 per cent of infections are spread by hands so we encourage

the boys by getting soap that they love (candy-scented is always a fave) and singing 'Happy Birthday' while they wash, which is the perfect amount of time

- Give them vitamin D supplements, especially if you live in the UK and between the months of October and April
- Puppy pads by the bed will save your carpets
- To get rid of the vomit smell from fabrics, once cleaned, spread bicarbonate of soda over the stain and leave for two hours before vacuuming up
- Once they start to recover, feed them BRAT to start: Bananas, Rice, Apple sauce and Toast
- Rehydration salts will aid recovery if they've been sick a lot. You can make ice lollies with them or mix up the salts as normal and start a 'Liquid Challenge' where they take a small syringe of just 5ml every five minutes. Over the course of an hour it adds up.

Final Word: *Not all of these routines will work for your household. But tweak them to suit your family and home, and you'll land on something that radically improves the manic mornings.*

Chapter 21

Co-ordinating the Extracurricular

So, you've got the homework headaches under control and the school run sorted. But what about the pile of life admin and juggling the never-ending after school activities which can make you feel like you're drowning?

At times, I'm basically a taxi service dropping one child off at football and then picking another one up from gymnastics before taking the third to a birthday party. It's regularly a logistical nightmare – I'm sure you can relate.

As parents, we are constantly being pulled in so many different directions and that house of cards I mentioned right at the start of this book is just as apparent when it comes to the extracurricular activities.

We're going to look at practical ways to manage their busy social lives and how to have a semblance of one yourself! But, most importantly, we'll talk about how to find some balance to make sure you're not stretching yourself too thin. You can't do everything. And that's OK!

Important Information Album

I would be lost without my phone because it holds so much information. I've created a photo album on there with pictures of school events, school dinner menus, party invitations, the Wi-Fi password, a photo of inside each of the kids' shoes to remember their sizes, which is a super easy way of making sure that a) important info isn't lost and b) I can locate it quickly.

Create a Home Command Centre

This is basically a place where I keep all kinds of useful info: our family calendar, the kids' chore charts, our meal plan, any birthday party invites and a school checklist so that I can keep track of clubs and everything the kids need to take to school on a daily basis. My 'command centre' is made of wipeable acrylic so I can use whiteboard markers to add notes and info and it helps to keep the whole family organised as well as my stress levels low.

Family Calendars

There are so many great apps out there that sync up your schedules and avoid any clashes which will rock the routine. The best ones are colour-coded by family members and really simple to use.

Get Your Party On

Whether you're hosting at home or hiring a venue, planning a children's birthday party is full on, so thank goodness they only come round once a year!

The three things I'd recommend most for having a successful party are:

1. The day before, text your invitees with a friendly reminder that the party is tomorrow and that you're really looking forward to seeing them.
2. If the party is at a venue, don't forget to take candles for the cake, a lighter and a knife to cut it with.
3. Take a few extra party bags just in case you get some unexpected additional guests in the form of siblings or people who haven't RSVPd but turn up anyway (grrrr!).

Present Stash

Keep a box of gifts which you can dip into for birthday parties and it's one less thing to have to remember to sort. Make sure your stash stays fully stocked by picking up items on special offers throughout the year. The middle aisles of budget supermarkets are also excellent sources of interesting, well-made but inexpensive children's gifts. I'd also recommend regifting when you end up with a duplicate present. Just make sure you don't gift it back to the original giver!

WhatsApp Groups

OK, the pinging might sometimes make you want to throw your phone across the living room, but WhatsApp groups have, on the whole, made our lives so much easier to manage. I've often relied on my class groups to check things about homework or to be reminded that they need £1 for a non-uniform day and they're great for arranging playdates and teacher gifts as well. I've also needed them for emergencies like the time I had to ask someone to pick the kids up for me when I'd locked myself out of the house with my car keys inside. Eek!

The best class groups I've been part of are the ones that stick to the purpose they were created for – to share and communicate useful information about the school and related activities. With so many different people on there, they can sometimes diverge from that original purpose and when they do, I'd say it's best to avoid getting involved in gossip or discussions criticising the school or individual teachers.

And if the pinging gets too much but you don't want to leave the group, remember you don't have to have notifictions on! Turning off phone notifications is a small way of reclaiming some headspace back. Or if that's not an option for you, mute it for a while and revel in the peace.

Car Pooling

If there's an opportunity to share the dropping and picking up from various clubs with another family, seize it!

Teacher Gifts

A while ago I made a video on end-of-term gifts and did a poll of teachers to see what they actually wanted. The overwhelming response was that they preferred gift vouchers to wine, chocolates or mugs. But another thing to come out of my bit of market research was that they genuinely love receiving cards with heartfelt messages inside and they do keep them because they're so personal and special.

Meal Plan to Suit the Schedule

If you're going to be out late, make sure you've got something ready prepared or quick on your meal planner. Our busiest night is a Thursday because the boys have all got clubs after school and then there's a teeny tiny window before they go to Scouts or Cubs, so that's the evening they get pasta, pesto and tuna.

Swap Baths for Showers

Doing this speeds up the whole bathtime routine no end and also saves water. My boys love a bath bomb but I found you can also get shower bombs which you put in the bottom of your shower tray and they give off this amazing scent. Anything that encourages them not to be soap dodgers, right?

Fill up a Flask

Don't forget yourself in all this! If you're going to be standing on the touchline of an under nines' football match for an hour, make time to prepare yourself a flask or thermal mug of tea or coffee to help see you through. Especially when it's in the depths of winter.

En Route Spelling Tests

On the evenings you're on a really tight schedule, use the dead time on the journey going from A to B to practise that week's spelling test or times tables. It's a better option than trying to cram it in when you're back at home and their energy levels have crashed and disappeared for the day.

Cushion the Timetable

Just as we discussed in the previous chapter with the school run, build in contingency time to take care of unforeseen circumstances. Otherwise you're setting yourself up for a torrid experience when there's a traffic jam, a forgotten water bottle you've got to go back for or a parking space you can't find.

Take Advantage

If you've got a half hour swimming lesson to sit through before you're up and at it again, treat it as 'Me Time'. It's a chance to stop, sit down and switch off. Granted, the public swimming pool doesn't quite conjure up the same vibe as a luxury spa (!) but you can block out the din by listening to a podcast, which means you can still keep a beady eye on how your child's backstroke is coming along.

Night Out Nightmares

Every class group needs an organiser. When someone else takes on that role, I always think 'thank goodness!' because it has occasionally ended up being me and it's not an easy job! If it's you, my advice would be that when there's a night out being planned, avoid getting bogged down in long discussions about who can do what date and instead, immediately set up a poll. Put your date options in, share the link and people tick which ones they can make. Choose the date most can do and stick to it.

Banish the Guilt

If you can't make a dance class, drama group or swimming lesson now and again, guess what? It doesn't matter. Sometimes life takes over and something has to give. Don't ever feel guilty – your child is loved and supported and isn't going to suffer from having missed the odd after–school class.

Use the Breaks to Reassess

When the swimming lessons, football, gymnastics, trampolining or whatever else stop for the school holidays, it's a good time to reassess everything. Take advantage of the pause to look at the schedule and decide if there's anything you could do with letting go of. Or, if it's possible, swapping to a different day. You'll know how manageable it's been over the previous term and where all the pinch points are, so really consider whether you could do with relieving any of the pressures.

The children can also use these breaks to figure out what they really want to do. In our house, Caleb was so much more interested in theatre than playing football and giving him the space to think about what he was passionate about helped him decide what he wanted to drop and to pursue instead.

The Covid lockdowns also gave our family a chance to look at all the things we were doing and once everything started opening back up again, there were quite a few activities we just didn't go back to. If the kids hadn't mentioned it or missed it, we cut it out of the schedule.

Moment for you

Take a Rest Night

If you're like me and you find it hard to sit down and relax because there's *always* something that needs doing, then you definitely need a 'rest night'.

Give yourself an easy night in terms of both the evening meal and the kids, so in our house that means a movie night and an easy dinner – pancakes, a takeaway, a buffet grazing board or a picnic in front of the TV. Keep it as simple and as quick as possible and don't feel a single shred of guilt.

Final Word: Learn to say no. If the karate class is on the other side of town and would mean busting a gut to make it on time, or the gymnastics club finishes late and would make it difficult to find time for dinner, or the golf sessions are just too expensive, you don't have to do it. This is a good lesson for your child, too if you explain why you're saying no and frame it as what comes with being part of a family. It's giving yourself the permission to stop or find another way – instead of the pricey golf lessons, perhaps have the odd Saturday afternoon at the local driving range.

It's also worth remembering that as well as not overburdening yourself, kids need downtime to unwind too. So take your foot off the gas (sometimes literally!) and stay home.

V:
Everything I've Learned About . . .

Phew! I feel like we've covered a lot of ground and I hope you've found a lot to take away from what I've shared so far in this book.

But I've been a mum for 13 years now and I know there are some issues that can't be solved with a quick fix – they are the same worries and fears we all have but when you're caught in the middle of them, they can sometimes feel insurmountable.

So I wanted to dedicate this final part of the book to some of my personal journeys and experiences and how we worked through them. I guess these are the chapters I wish I'd been able to read when I was an exhausted new mum, convinced I was getting everything wrong and having long forgotten what a night of unbroken sleep felt like.

Whether it's sleep issues, potty training, boundary pushing or how to handle the upheaval becoming parents brings to your relationship with your partner, I'm going to tell you some of the tips and techniques that helped get us through the tougher times. They won't all be 'right' for your family, but there may be some elements you can take away and adapt to suit your set up.

More than anything, I want to offer you my solidarity and reassurance that things will get easier. We've got this.

Chapter 22

Sleep

My kids are all old enough to have given us the gift of sleep again (thank you, boys!), but I can vividly remember the days when I was so tired my whole body ached. I will never take sleep for granted again.

I found it really difficult the first time around. Like, breaking point difficult. Fraser was the first baby on both sides of our family, so I had no real experience and didn't have a clue about what life with a newborn would be like. We were lucky if we got a two-hour stretch of sleep from him and I felt permanently wired.

It was like another level of tiredness to the point of being delirious and I remember little things would set me off on a spiral. If Matt said the wrong thing, I'd be super emotional. I wasn't very good at sleeping when the baby slept (everyone tells you to do this, but it's not as easy as it sounds) and I remember pushing the pram up the high street one day and just crying from pure exhaustion. It sounds ridiculous now, but I used to put on a baby-gro which said 'I love mummy' so I'd be reminded of that and given a little boost when woken for a breastfeed or nappy change in the middle of the night!

I don't claim to be an expert on sleep, but having been through this three times now, I have picked up a bit of knowledge along the way and this is what (eventually) worked for us.

238

Co-sleeping

I know bed-sharing isn't for everyone, but we've always done it and it was often how our whole house got the most sleep. Even now it's not unusual for one of them to have wandered in and snuggled up at some point during the night. If they're sleeping better, then I'm sleeping better and if it suits you and your partner then I'd say just go with it.

When they were babies, we had a co-sleeper cot which attached to the side of the bed, but they would also come in with me quite a lot, following the guidance for safe bed-sharing from lullabytrust.org.uk which is as follows:

- Keep pillows and adult bedding away from your baby
- Make sure you and your partner have not had any alcohol or taken medication which induces sleepiness
- Neither partner should be a smoker
- Baby should be placed on their back to the side of mum, not in between the adults in the bed
- Co-sleeping should always take place in a bed, never on a sofa or armchair

Routine

Finding a good routine is one of the things that makes me most happy in life! I've made so many routine videos over the years that I think just about everything is covered – even Kiki our dog.

For little ones, I've found that introducing a gentle routine from about eight weeks is really helpful, but it's so important that you don't force it and end up tearing your hair out because your baby didn't get the memo . . .

Some books made me feel bad that my baby wasn't following

the rigid routine the author had set out, so I found a more relaxed way of doing things and then constantly adjusted it as they got older. I based it loosely on *The 48-Hour Baby Sleep Solution* by Angela Lawson, but kept everything flexible as there will always be days where teething, growth spurts, sickness or just general uncooperativeness inevitably get in the way!

You can find my typical daily routines for 3–6 months, 6–9 months and 9–12 months at the end of this chapter (see page 247).

Self-Settling

I definitely veer more towards the gentle parenting model and so at first, the idea of teaching my babies to 'self-settle' made me a little nervous. But after a lot of thought (and a whole lot of lost sleep!) we decided to try it with Fraser when he was about nine months old and I came to see it as helping him learn a valuable skill.

While it's lovely watching your baby fall asleep on the breast, for Fraser it meant that he found it difficult or even impossible to go to sleep any other way. Because he'd formed a sleep association with feeding, when he woke up and the boob he'd fallen asleep on wasn't there anymore, he couldn't soothe himself back again.

Now, I know lots of mums are more than happy to continue feeding to sleep, but when I was on my knees with tiredness, I needed to break that cycle and help Fraser to settle himself. So, I resolved to stop putting him down asleep in the evenings and I'd even take him out of the darkened room where we'd been feeding into the light again, so he'd be sleepy but awake before placing him in the cot.

He didn't like it at first. Not at all. I would leave the room for one minute before going back in to reassure him that I was still there by stroking his back but resisting the temptation to pick him up.

The first night we tried, it took around 40 minutes of this back and forth until he eventually went to sleep on his own, but we got a six-hour stretch after that which was unheard of at that point. The second night it took around 20 minutes and by the third night we'd cracked it and he was putting himself to sleep having gone down awake. Again, I have to reiterate this was our experience and certainly won't be the case for every baby.

With Caleb and Jackson, I put them down sleepy but awake from day dot, so they knew what to do. It wasn't always plain-sailing, it's not a magic solution to every sleep issue you'll encounter as a mum and I know it won't be what everyone wants to do, but that's our story and it was life-changing for us.

Naps

I wish I could go back and tell myself to quit being so hung up on the whole nap routine. With my first I was obsessed with getting him napping in his crib at home in a quiet darkened room which I can see now was making life harder for myself. Because a nap in a car seat, a sling or a buggy is still a nap. It's not the end of the world if they're not in their cot. And once you have a second child, you really have to take your naps wherever you can find them . . .

I'd also say that having them nap on you while you sit on the couch doing absolutely nothing is vastly underrated and something we don't allow ourselves to appreciate enough. It's pretty blissful and not a stage that lasts all that long, so savour it while it does.

Babywearing

I started using a sling day to day with my second and it was such a godsend. I wish I'd done it with Fraser because Caleb and Jackson both loved it – it was an instant comforter and sleep solution which saved me a nap battle and also allowed me to be hands-free to get on with other things while they soundly slept. We started off with a soft stretchy sling which cocoons them so beautifully and then as they got a bit older moved to a structured baby carrier. I babywore for as long as I possibly could and Matt did too.

If you're new to babywearing, there are local sling libraries all over the country where you can try out all the different kinds and brands to see what suits you best as well as getting expert advice on how to use them safely.

Four-Month Sleep Regression

Yes, this is a real thing. Just when you're settling into a bit of a routine and think you've found your groove – bam! – at around four months, all hell breaks loose and you feel like you're back to square one. I promise you, you're not. This is all very normal and is (yet another) phase that will pass.

The best thing I found with all my boys at this stage was to go with the flow and to accept that the routine was going to need some bend and flex for a couple of weeks or so. I rode it out by doing lots of baby massage after baths and tried to keep any noise from the rest of the house away from where we were settling down.

It's also reassuring to look at these stages as developmental rather than 'regressions'. The word regression has such negative connotations, so reframing the situation helps you see a bigger, more positive picture.

Sleeping Bags

Baby sleeping bags are always top of my shopping list for little ones, especially from around six months when they're moving around a lot more and would kick off a normal cover. If you've not seen them, they clip over your baby's shoulders so you know they're going to be safe, snuggly and warm throughout the night. They come in different togs so you can get thinner ones for summer and thicker ones for when it gets colder during the winter. They're also perfect for keeping your baby warm if you're bed-sharing and need to keep your duvet tucked away.

Comforters

I introduced comforters for all my boys from pretty much the first week. All of them had a soft blanket and a little bunny toy which they slept with and because these items looked, felt and smelled so familiar, they brought calm and were very useful tools to have. The panic when you realise you've mislaid blankie or bunny, though ... that's intense! A friend of mine even resorted to sewing a tracker device into a cuddly toy's tummy so she could track him down, the fear of him getting lost was so strong. If you can buy an identical comforter and keep it in reserve as a secret substitute, I'd recommend that.

Don't Forget Yourself

It's all too easy as mums to put ourselves to the bottom of the priority list and forget that we need taking care of as well. But even when you're in the middle of the sleepless nights madness, there are lots of things we can do to make those challenges easier to cope with.

Make sure you're having a good, healthy breakfast every morning and getting out and about regularly for fresh air – a walk can make the world of difference. I also found that having a shower (even if it was only the two-minuite, straight in-and-out kind!) and putting on a bit of makeup always made me feel a bit more human and not as much in a slump.

Take healthy, energy-releasing snacks with you when you're out the house, especially when you're visiting the soft play where it's impossible to get anything non-stodgy. I found cutting down on my coffee really helped my energy levels which sounds counterintuitive because you assume caffeine will make you more awake. In those early days, it was actually making me more anxious and affecting what little sleep I was managing to get.

Setting a bedtime for myself was another good tip. The hours kind of merge into each other so I'd suddenly realise it was 11.30pm and kick myself for not having gone to bed two hours earlier.

And my final tip is to power nap. Research shows that 20 minutes is the ideal amount of napping time – it's just enough to experience drifting off and the brain slowing down, but you're not in the deep REM sleep which means you wake up groggy and probably feeling even worse than you did before.

Accepting Help

If I could do it all again, I would ask for help a lot sooner. I'd admit I was struggling and let someone come in and take over while I slept. I'd let the washing pile up and not worry about the mess, just for those first few months, and get some sleep instead. However high your standards are, you need to lower them when you have a baby. Visitors come to see you, not to inspect the dust on your mantelpiece.

And be specific when asking for that help – tell people what you need them to do otherwise it won't get done.

I get asked a lot about the routines I used with the boys when they were little and so thought it would be useful to share them with you here. I have to say, these were never set in stone and we had to be prepared to adapt them or ditch them all together when circumstances changed. But this is how I generally aimed to schedule my days. I should also add that I got into the habit of changing the nappy every time I fed.

3–6 months

7–7.30am:	Wake and feed
8.30am:	Nap
10am:	Wake and feed
12–2pm:	Nap
2pm:	Wake and feed
4.30pm:	Nap
6–6.30pm:	Bath time
7pm:	Feed and bedtime

6–9 months

7am:	Wake and milk feed
8am:	Breakfast (solids)
9am:	Nap
10am:	Awake and play
11.30:	Lunch (solids)
12pm:	Milk feed and nap

2pm:	Wake and milk feed
4.30pm:	Optional nap
5pm:	Dinner (solids)
6pm:	Bathtime
6.30–7pm:	Milk feed and bedtime

9–12 months

7am:	Wake and milk feed
7.30–8am:	Breakfast
9am:	Nap (lots of babies start to drop this one from around 10 months – sorry!)
10am:	Wake and snack
11.30–12pm:	Lunch
12.30–2pm:	Nap
3pm:	Optional milk feed
4.30–5pm:	Dinner
6pm:	Bath time
6.30pm:	Milk feed
7pm:	Bedtime

Final Word: *If you're currently battling through sleep deprivation, hang on in there. It might not feel like it right now, but this isn't forever. Try not to compare your little one to others – all babies are different. Don't be swayed either by what friends, family members or certain books tell you that your baby 'should' be doing. There is no 'should' here – nothing is permanent and you and your little one will figure a way through.*

Chapter 23

Potty Training

I started potty training Fraser at two years and two months and ended up putting heaps of unnecessary pressure on myself — it became an extra stress that we really could have done without. It's very easy to become influenced by other mums in your NCT group or local playgroup who might be comparing potty training notes, but try not to get drawn into all that. Potty training shouldn't feel like a stressful process. It can be quite an exciting next step if you allow it to unfold when your child is ready. Don't let it drive you, well, potty!

In this chapter we'll look at how to tell when it's time and some of the fun tricks that I found helped us once we'd started our journey.

Know When They're Ready

It's pointless starting to potty train before your child is ready and there are some key signs to watch out for when it comes to this. The first is when they start telling you they've gone for a wee in their nappy as it shows they're becoming aware of 'going'.

By the time they're telling you they need a wee or are even pointing to the changing bag before they go, knowing they'll need a fresh nappy shortly, you can be quite confident that they're ready for the next stage.

Another sign is them becoming much more interested in the toilet and showing some curiosity in you or (if they have any) their older siblings going.

Don't Be Afraid to Stop

I'd say if you've been at it for three or four days and don't feel you're making much progress or any at all, it's probably too soon for your little one. Give yourself a break, abandon the operation and come back to it a bit further down the line and you may find that with a few more months on the clock and having already laid a bit of the groundwork, you get it cracked straight away. They may even skip the potty stage all together and head straight for the loo.

Get Them Involved

I've found that making kids feel like they're very much part of the process goes a long way. With Jackson, we went online and he got to choose his own potty and the big boy pants that he liked – he really enjoyed being involved in those decisions. We also had some children's story books centred around potty training which we started reading a few weeks before beginning and were a big help in engaging his interest.

Some of the books we found especially good:

Peek-a-Poo by Guido van Genechten
The Little Princess: I Want My Potty! by Tony Ross
Pirate Pete's Potty by Andrea Pinnington
Boys' Potty Time by Dawn Sirett

Praise and Reward

Every time the boys made it to the potty in time, it was a cause for celebration and we'd make a big deal of praising them. As a reward they'd get a sticker for pees and a chocolate button for poos which were, for obvious reasons, worth a bit more!

Open Door Policy

We tried to 'demystify' going to the toilet whenever we were potty training and had an open-door policy so they could wander in and see me, Matt or siblings on the loo. Showing that it's a normal process for everyone and that it's fine to be curious helped spark interest.

Stay Home

It's not always possible to do but if you can, I'd really advise dedicating a couple of days where you don't leave the house. It's much easier to pick up any cues and it also doesn't matter as much when they have the inevitable accidents.

Waterproof Shoes

These are essentials for when you go out and about because accidents *do* happen and they're a lot easier to cope with if you don't need to change the shoes as well. I'd also take a change of top for myself because said accidents seemed to have a habit of happening while they were positioned on my hip.

Number Twos

It's very common for kids to have nailed the wees but take longer to feel comfortable doing poos in the potty. That's totally understandable when you think about it – they're used to the nappy 'catching' the poo, so psychologically it feels as if they're losing part of themselves and that can feel very scary.

We helped bridge this transitional period by lining the potty with a nappy and sometimes even putting the nappy back on them again when they signalled they needed a poo, but were getting upset about the prospect of going in the potty.

There's a really sweet, simple story on YouTube and various websites called 'Poo Goes to Poo Land' which is aimed at helping children with their anxiety over this. It tells the tale from the perspective of the character 'Poo' and him needing to get home to Poo Land where his family are waiting for him. But he needs the little boy in the story Ollie to send him down the toilet to get there. It's so engaging and perfectly pitched and I know a lot of parents have reached a breakthrough after reading it with their children.

Pull-Ups at Night

Staying dry overnight will usually take a fair bit longer than the potty training so take it one step at a time and use pull-ups through the night.

Dream Wee

We used to take the boys for a 'dream wee' when we went to bed at about 11pm. We'd carry them half sleeping from bed, put them on the toilet for the wee and then pop them back to bed again having barely woken them up. It's a bit like dream feeding, which I know a lot of people like to do with babies to fill them up with milk last thing at night to try and avoid a wake up in the small hours.

Reframe Your Questions

Rather than continually asking your child if they need a wee or a poo, instead remind them regularly that they can tell you when they want to go. This puts them in control of the situation rather than having them feel like they're being bombarded with the same question over and over again.

Magic Stickers

You can pick these up all over the internet and they're such a clever way of making potty trips fun. Stick one at the bottom of the bowl and when your child pees, a mystery picture appears. This can also help with the aim, which any parent of boys will agree is an essential life skill for them!

Target Practice

While we're on the topic of aim, we also used a few Cheerios in the toilet bowl when the boys migrated from the potty to stand-up wees in the loo. I'm not saying they're perfect but every little helps.

Final Word: *The most important thing to remember with potty training is that kids will all get there in the end. When they're 18 and going for a job interview, no one is going to ask them at what age they stopped wearing nappies. Well, it would be pretty weird if they did!*

Chapter 24

Post-Baby Relationships

I'm pretty sure I asked Matt on our first date if he wanted children or not. I know that might sound a little extreme, but I'd always wanted to be a mum – it was this deep-seated, burning desire for me and I didn't see the point in falling for someone who wasn't on the same page.

Luckily, a future with children was just as important to him as it was for me and when we went travelling together, about six months into our relationship, we were already talking about baby names. By our first wedding anniversary, I was five months pregnant with Fraser who was named after Fraser Island in Australia where we'd visited on our travels. So we didn't muck around!

However, no matter how strong your relationship is or how much you know and love each other, I don't think anything can prepare you for the massive shock of bringing a baby into the equation.

Of course it's a time of great joy and excitement, but it will also probably rock the very foundations you've built together and test you as a couple over and over again. At the time, Matt was just starting up a new business and Fraser was born near to Christmas which was his busiest period. It meant he was pretty much back to work the day after I gave birth, which made those first few weeks even more intense. And, I can hardly believe this now, but two weeks after Fraser was born we moved house! What were we thinking?!

I'd be lying if I said our relationship didn't come under strain during that crazy time. Having a newborn is all-consuming and the sheer exhaustion sometimes makes you say things in frustration that you don't mean and later regret. But I knew we'd come through it and I love Matt a million times more now because he is such a great dad to our kids. Plus, he's seen me at my absolute worst and yet he still loves me!

Hopefully you'll find some of these tips helpful (all compiled with the benefit of hindsight!) and Matt has added a few words from his perspective, too. He says he's the fourth most important man in my life these days. And he's absolutely right!

There's no secret formula for the perfect relationship but with a dollop of compromise, a generous sprinkling of understanding and a healthy dose of humour, you won't go far wrong.

Tell Each Other What You Need

Communication is key. In the first few weeks after having Fraser, I used to look at Matt and think, 'why don't you just *know*?' But he was learning too, and obviously (because he's not a mind reader) he needed me to tell him what I wanted him to help me with. It might have been taking the baby for a walk around the park to give me a precious half hour to myself, or making me a cup of tea because the last one had gone cold before I'd had a chance to drink it, or fetching me a clean muslin while I was pinned to the sofa breastfeeding a hungry baby – I only had to tell him rather than simmering silently that he didn't instinctively know.

That applies to the bigger things, too. Keep talking to each other about how you're feeling, what you're worried about and the emotional support you need as you navigate this brave new world.

How Partners Can Support Breastfeeding

I know a lot of partners worry about what their role is in the early weeks, especially if the mum is exclusively breastfeeding. But there is SO much they can do.

Matt took charge of the winding – very good he was at it, too! – and that became his job while I rested following a mammoth cluster feeding session. He was also chief nappy changer, did lots of skin to skin and was responsible for bathtimes and I know he felt this one-on-one time was very bonding.

And of course, a hugely important part of your partner's duties during breastfeeding is to support YOU, both practically (with household chores, meal prep, making sure the remote is within easy reach) and emotionally to help you achieve whatever your nursing goals are.

It's Not a Competition

When you're tired and run-down, it's so easy to feel resentment towards your partner who you might see as having the better deal. Matt would come home from work with all these stories about what he'd done and who he'd had lunch with and all I had to share with him was the colour of Fraser's poo that day.

To me, Matt seemed to assume maternity leave was about going and meeting my NCT friends for coffee. I actually remember him once joking to me that 'maternity leave equals coffee!' and I wanted to punch him in the face!

As long as you're sharing the load as best you can, then it's pointless trying to work out whose life is harder or comparing notes about who's the most tired. Competitive tiredness is a conversation that will rarely end well.

For us, 50/50 parenting meant Matt's winding duties continuing through the night. Sure, he had to be up for work in the morning, but so did I. Looking after a baby is just as much a full-time job as running a business. We had a night-time system in place, which meant I would feed the baby and then nudge Matt awake to burp, change and put back in the cot we had attached to the bed.

United Front

Having the same values plays a huge part in successful parenting and your relationship. Matt and I have always agreed on things like discipline and how we want to encourage and support the boys to reach their potential. And when there has been a bit of, shall we say 'debate' about how to handle certain situations, we don't have those discussions in front of the kids. We are always stronger together.

Date Nights

Obviously while you have young kids, date nights can't be what they used to be. There are no spontaneous evenings in the pub, trips to the cinema or wild nights clubbing. But I always thought it was important to carve out what time we could devote to being a couple, even if that just meant having a takeaway at home or watching a movie together on the sofa. So we did our best to schedule this whenever we could.

Granted, even the simplest of plans are at risk of being scuppered when there are little ones in the house, but those times Matt and I managed an 'at home' date night felt precious and helped us find each other and reconnect in the middle of all the madness. Even if we did end up spending the whole time talking about and looking at photos of the kids!

Adult Space

I can never totally switch off when I'm surrounded by piles of toys and plastic clutter. I used to envy people who had a playroom they could simply close the door on, forgetting about the mess behind it! Whatever your house situation, creating an adult space or toy-free zone for the evenings can help you reset and relax together at the end of the day.

It's one of the reasons I started my evening cleaning routine and is also why we've always had a set bath time of 6pm for the boys so Matt and I get that bit of time for ourselves.

Achieving that adult space comes back to what we discussed on page 83 about everything having a place. It might be as basic as chucking all the toys into baskets, as long as they are cleared out of the way and there's an area of your living space that you can reclaim at the end of each day.

Flirt With Each Other

Receiving an unexpected flirty text message from your partner can perk up a drab day and put a pep in your step! It only takes a minute to tell someone you love them and are thinking of them and being reminded of that when you're changing your ump-teenth dirty nappy of the day is never a bad thing.

Sleep on It

I know the advice tends to be never go to sleep on an argument, but I've found that parking the disagreement and agreeing to discuss it in the morning means you wake up with cooler heads making it easier to resolve. It sometimes means it's blown over completely because after a few hours' rest, you both realise it doesn't really matter anymore.

Find the Humour

Laughter in a relationship is everything to me. Matt is quite witty with a quick sense of humour and he's able to see the funny side of most things. Even baby sick! His humour always puts things into perspective and if you have the sort of relationship where you can make each other laugh, you're winning.

Little Acts of Kindness

Some of you might have read the best-selling book *The 5 Love Languages: The Secret to Love That Lasts* by Gary Chapman. And if you haven't, you should definitely check it out. It includes a personal profile assessment so you can discover the 'love language' of you and your partner (acts of service, gifts, physical touch, quality time or words of affirmation), which will help you both show and receive love in a more meaningful way.

According to the questionnaire, Matt's love language is acts of service, so preparing his favourite meal is literally the best thing ever as far as he's concerned. One Father's Day I cleaned out the garage for him and he was over the moon about it! That sort of thing means more to him than an expensive gift. My love language is physical touch so I'm happy with a cuddle on the sofa or a back rub.

These little acts of thoughtfulness that you know your partner responds positively to, can make such a big difference.

Intimacy

I'm not necessarily talking about between the sheets here because what happens there is personal and individual to every couple. But we try to remember to give each other kisses 'hello' and 'goodbye' and the odd squeeze of the bum or waist now and again. Any form of touch helps maintain connection.

I asked Matt if he could add a few words about how he saw his role as a dad and partner and how he thought our relationship changed after babies. Over to him:

'I remember Emily and Fraser being discharged from the hospital when he was about eight hours old and I couldn't believe we were being allowed to leave with this tiny baby. As first-time parents we really didn't have a clue what we were doing and it felt mad that we were expected to go home and just get on with it.

It was scary, but as a new dad you have to step up very quickly and I knew my job was to be there for Emily. She'd been through the pregnancy, birth and was now juggling the breastfeeding day and night and so I had to be responsible for everything else.

I know dads can sometimes feel a bit helpless in the early days, but there is so much to do and while the mum focuses on the baby, we can take charge in other areas. It's about batch cooking freezer meals and keeping on top of the cleaning and tidying. It's

about changing nappies, winding, bathing, soothing, rocking and walking with the pram.

Everyone says it, but nothing can prepare you for sleep deprivation until you have children. You might have pulled all-nighters in your youth, but you won't have done months upon months of surviving on two or three hours of sleep a night. But I knew that Emily had it even tougher because she was doing all the feeding.

My top advice to new dads is don't be selfish. Put mum first. Ask her what she needs and do it. When you have children together, you have to be there for each other during the highs and the lows and generally it makes people love each other even more. It did for us.

I'd also say to make sure you take photos of mum and baby. Capture those really candid moments, the ones which you'll both be able to look back on in years to come and recognise as a truly special time. All too often people end up with loads of pictures of visitors holding the baby and hardly any of the mum.

Oh, and a word to the wise. Bear in mind that when you come out the other side and life is feeling a bit more normal and manageable, that's exactly the point when your wife starts to get maternal again . . . just saying!'

Final Word: *It's inevitable that your relationship will change as your worlds turn upside down and you go through the biggest and most life-changing transition you're likely to encounter, but when it's time to come up for air again, you can emerge stronger and more of a team than ever before.*

Chapter 25

Baby Life

Newborns are adorable squishy little things, but you've probably realised by now that they don't come with an instruction manual. And given the fact that babies don't typically smile until they're six weeks old, becoming a mum is a bit like having a very demanding boss who gives you no praise or reward in return for your toils.

I thought this would be a good place to compile my all-time favourite baby hacks in one place. So that's what you've got, right here in this chapter!

FEEDING

Which Boob?

If you're breastfeeding and struggle to remember which side you last fed from, put a clip on your left or right bra strap or a hair band on your wrist to remind you. There are loads of fancy apps out there for breastfeeding, but I find the simplest ways are the most effective.

Feeding Necklace

When babies get beyond the first few months, they start to get a little more curious during feeds and often like to grab fistfuls of your hair or become distracted by what's going on elsewhere in the room. A feeding or nursing necklace made from non-toxic beads is such a good invention – you wear it during feeds and it helps your baby focus on the task at hand and gives them something to play with that isn't going to make you yelp in pain!

One Up One Down Method

If you're breastfeeding, there's no need to replace your wardrobe with clothes specifically made for nursing – just use stretchy vests underneath your usual tops. When you lift your top up, pull the vest down and latch your baby on. Your tummy is covered by the bottom half of the vest, the top of your boob is covered by your top and any other flesh is covered by baby's head, so if you're breastfeeding in public and feeling a bit self-conscious, it's really discreet.

Feeding Activity Basket

If you're feeding a newborn and have an older child, an activity box is the way forward. When you sit down to feed, knowing you're going to be stuck on the sofa for a while, you can play with your older one from the contents of the box. Include small age-appropriate toys, activity books, stickers and favourite story books and keep them on rotation every few days to hold their interest. It means your older child never feels left out because instead, it becomes special reading time with mummy. You can also add in some supplies for yourself like breast pads, nipple cream and a bottle of water.

Hang Bibs on Highchairs

Stick an adhesive hook to the back of your highchair and you've got a convenient place to store your bibs once they're washed.

Bananas for Weaning

Bananas are a great first food for babies, but they're so slippery. I used to make it easier to grip by leaving the skin on – first slicing the banana in half across the middle and then slicing about an inch off the skin. Another way to give your baby more control is to separate the banana into three finger-sized sections. Gently push your forefinger down on the tip of the banana and it will naturally split into three segments which are the perfect size for little hands.

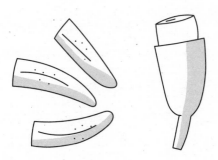

CHANGING

Navigating Newborn Nappies

While you're waiting for the umbilical stump to drop off (it normally takes a week or two), it's a little fiddly to fasten nappies as the stump needs to remain exposed. I found making two little diagonal cuts in the waist trim made the nappy really easy to fold down around the stump.

Also, I didn't realise at first, but in order to tell if a nappy is wet and needs changing, look at the yellow stripe on the outside. If it's turned blue, then it's wet. Clever!

Frill Seekers

Make sure you pull out the frilly bits of the nappy around your baby's legs. If they're left folded or tucked in then you'll end up getting leaks.

Little Wrigglers

When changing a dirty nappy, keep baby's clothing clean and little hands contained by bringing the back of the buttoned vest over one shoulder. Then fold the front flap up to meet the back and button them together with baby's arms contained in what is a makeshift sling.

Changing Caddy

In the early days I made a nappy changing caddy to keep in the living room or kitchen for quick, convenient nappy changes. They sell lovely ones online with lots of useful compartments, but

I just used a basket or box and added nappies, wipes, barrier cream, a change of clothes and a muslin.

Rubber Band Trick

Secure a rubber band around your pack of wet wipes, right next to the opening of the pack and make sure that it is pretty snug. When you pull out a wipe, only one will come out rather than a long connecting trail of them.

Coconut Oil

Babies can have quite dry skin, but coconut oil really helps to moisturise it. Just put some on a cotton wool ball or cloth and gently rub in. I used to add some to a small reusable tub to use when we were out.

Baby Boys

It's a strange phenomenon, but boys have a tendency to pee like a water fountain as soon as their nappy is removed. Place a new nappy over the groin while cleaning their bum and this will keep it all contained and stop everything in the vicinity from getting a soaking.

Also, make sure the penis is pointing down when you put the nappy on otherwise you're going to get a sprinkler over the top.

BATH & BED

Room Temperature

Babies get colder than you think, so I downloaded a little chart which showed how many layers they should wear in what temperature. You could print one out as well and keep it pinned to the nursery wall. The best temperature for your baby's bath is 37°C and for their bedroom it's 19°C.

Hot Water Bottle Warmer

If your baby hates being put down in the cot, first of all know this is really normal. I mean, if you were having a lovely cuddle with your favourite person and all of a sudden they decided to cut short that snuggle and leave you by yourself, you'd be pretty mad about it too! But sometimes the transfer from your arms to the cot is disrupted because the cot isn't as welcoming and warm as you are. Putting a hot water bottle into the cot for 15 minutes before the transfer so they're not being placed down on a cold sheet can avoid that rude awakening.

Teething Problems

It's so hard for them when their little teeth start coming through. To help ease their discomfort, I would put some apple sauce or other fruit purée into the middle of a flannel, close it up with an elastic band and then freeze it. When their teeth are causing them upset, you'll have something sweet and cold for them to chew on and soothe those poor gums.

Bath Toys

Anyone who has looked inside kids' bath toys will know how stomach-churningly gross they get with black mould. I use my hot glue gun to seal up the little hole in the backs and bottoms of the toys – they can still float fine, but the water can't get in and they don't get all yucky.

Cotton Buds for Fingers

A wet cotton bud is very effective at cleaning in between new-born fingers and toes. It's amazing how much fluff and crusty milk they have nestling in the little creases.

Poorly Baby

If your baby is congested, a bowl of water under the radiator in their room will keep the air moist – you can even add a few drops of baby-friendly decongestant to the water. You might also take your baby in their Moses basket into the bathroom while the shower's on and the steam will help to clear their airways.

CLOTHES

Bundles of Joy

A great hack for going out is to make a clothing bundle that you can just throw in your baby bag so you've got a full change par-celled together. Lay out a baby vest or baby-gro folded in half lengthways and then place a pair of baby leggings (also folded lengthways) on top of it. Pop a pair of socks in the middle of your pile with the openings facing outwards and the toes touch-ing so your pile looks like a cross. Roll up the whole bundle and then pull the openings of the socks down over the top of either side and you have a full change of clothes all compact and ready to go. You could put this into a freezer bag so that you have somewhere to put the messy clothes afterwards.

Washing Socks

It is a truth universally acknowledged that at least one tiny baby sock will go missing in the machine with every wash. Don't ask me where they end up, but using mesh bags will keep them contained and stop them going astray while you wash them.

Envelope Shoulders

I mentioned this right at the start of the book because it's the discovery that got me into hacks in the first place. All baby vests and baby-gros are made with these clever envelope shoulders which allow you to slip the onesie downwards over your little one's legs rather than up and over their head – vital in the event of a poonami.

Final Word: The newborn phase is over faster than you could ever imagine. So hold them, kiss them, smell them and take as many photos and videos as you can because while the days are long, the years are so short.

Chapter 26

Boundary Pushing

I don't remember my eldest ever having tantrums, so they weren't really on my radar until Caleb, our second, came along. Oh boy, I certainly knew what they were after that!

As soon as he turned two, he started experiencing these huge emotions which would come out in sudden fits of temper and it was a shock to the system for all of us. Every situation had the potential to end in an outburst and he would scream and cry and protest with all his might, refusing to give in.

We would comfort ourselves by saying it was clearly a sign that he was going to be a CEO of a top company one day! Even now he's very strong-willed and stubborn, so it's definitely part of his make-up and as time has gone on, I've no doubt it will stand him in good stead in the future.

Caleb really is the most wonderful boy in a million different ways, but there were days when we found it incredibly hard and when it all kicked off, I had to find tactics to manage the situation, which I'm going to share with you in this chapter.

Something to bear in mind is that children will push boundaries when they feel safe and loved enough to do so. Kids lash out at home with you because they are secure in the knowledge that your love is unconditional and that means they feel able to test you. That's why they tend not to have the same sort of tantrums at nursery or when they're being looked after by other people. You know when you get reports of impeccable behaviour and wonder if there's been some sort of mistake and they've got the wrong child?

And like the sleep regression we talked about earlier, tantrums are developmental. I know they're exasperating and draining and make you want to kick and scream yourself, but they're not a reflection on you or your parenting or a sign that your child is being 'naughty' or 'manipulative'. Tantrums are how young children express that they're upset or frustrated while they're learning how to communicate with us.

Here are some strategies we used although they do come with a caveat – there's no catch-all solution and sometimes there's no choice but to hold your nerve and ride it out.

Pre-empt the Outburst

The best way to deal with a tantrum is surely to avoid it happening in the first place. That might sound a little weird, but by that I mean doing everything you can to steer clear of situations which can provoke one. For instance, turn down invites to parties or playdates which you know are going to clash with nap times or bed time – while you're in this 'phase' it's not worth putting yourself or your child through it.

If you sense that something is brewing, employ distraction techniques such as going outside and looking for aeroplanes and make sure you've always got snacks and age-appropriate toys to hand so you can divert attention quickly. Having their needs met means you can sometimes catch it before it escalates: mission accomplished, crisis averted.

Stay Calm

Although it might be tempting to shout, that's the very behaviour we're trying to teach them not to use. If you can, remain as calm and collected as possible throughout the tantrum – sometimes you might have to walk away and that's OK! There have been a few occasions where I've taken myself out of the situation, closed my eyes and counted to 10 before re-entering the room with a fresh head.

There are more tips on how to be a calmer parent at the end of this chapter.

Take Them Away From the Crowd

Removing them so they don't have an audience gives them a chance to calm down privately while they experience these big feelings. Just calmly pick them up without saying anything and walk away so they don't have any extra pressure of all eyes being on them.

Be Consistent With Your Rules

As hard as it is, stick to your guns and be consistent with your boundaries and house rules. So, no matter how ferocious the tantrum, nope, you're still not getting chocolate for breakfast!

When I'd warned the kids that we would leave wherever we were and whatever we were doing if the tantrum didn't stop, I knew I had to make good on that. I had to be willing to collect all our things very calmly, leave our friends and go home.

On the rare occasion that happened, it was hard because I never want to be the person who takes kids away from their fun, but my mum told me it was actually preparing for the future as well. I was doing this for them because I want them to be nice people who have respect for others. Hopefully when they're teenagers and Matt and I set a curfew of 11pm, they'll be back on the dot because they know that we mean what we say. Wishful thinking?

Give Them Choice

We had regular flashpoints with Caleb such as him objecting to the socks or trousers I was dressing him in or the snack I gave him. Making him feel like he had some say in these matters gave him a sense of autonomy, like he was the one making the decisions, and it worked so well.

I would give him a choice of outfits ('do you want to wear the green top or the yellow top?') or let him decide whether he had an apple or breadsticks as a snack and that would often evade a tantrum.

Practise Your Serious Voice

When we yell at our kids, it almost gives them permission to yell back at us and the situation can explode rather than defuse. I'd much rather talk to them with a serious, calm tone – I've always had quite a high-pitched voice, so this was something I had to do a lot of work on. I do have a much sterner voice that I can switch to when needed and the boys know for a fact I mean business when I do!

Hug It Out

Our little people experience these huge emotions that they don't really understand and sometimes all they need is a hug. While your instinct might be to get frustrated, putting your arms around them and soothing them through it might be the answer.

Just like every mum out there, I have bad days where I struggle. Anyone who says they don't is probably lying! But I try to parent calmly and choose grace over anger – there are a few things I do to keep everything on an even keel:

Don't Over Schedule

I definitely made this mistake as a new mum. I would book in all these meet-ups and activities in an attempt to fill the days and have lots of human connection. But trying to make it to all those arrangements on time would be a battle and by the time we got back home, I'd be absolutely whacked and certainly not the calm mama I wanted to be.

During maternity leave, I think it's much more realistic to schedule just one thing a day that gets you out of the house and that's it. Don't make a rod for your own back by being too ambitious. One activity is plenty and often achievement enough on its own.

Find Solutions

Identify the most stressful parts of the day and work out ways you can make them easier. If mornings are your most chaotic times, think about whether there's anything else you can get prepped the night before. Or if dinner times are a headache, perhaps more rigid meal planning or using your slow cooker will help you gain back a bit of control.

Breathing

I practised hypno-birthing with all of my labours and had a really good experience with it. I have used some of those techniques in day-to-day life since and I would say if it's getting tough and you feel like you're about to explode, take some time out. Walk away from your children (as long as they're safe) and breathe from your belly. Deep, slow breaths. They will notice you have gone and little silent gestures like walking out of the room while you regain composure, can be much more effective than shouting or arguing.

Create Routine

We've covered this a lot in the book, so you'll know that having routines helps me feel more in control of my life. I find it comforting and secure and that makes me calmer overall.

Me Time

This is so important, so make sure you ring-fence time for yourself. Have a dip into the 'Moments for You' I've scattered throughout this book for some ideas!

Grind Everything to a Halt

Trying to manage a disruption while juggling other things is guaranteed to send your stress levels through the roof, which is when I risk ending up shouting. Stopping whatever I'm doing in order to solely focus on the child who needs my attention makes a big statement without resorting to yelling and sometimes actions speak louder than words.

A really good example of this is when you're driving and trying to concentrate on the road, but the kids are fighting or asking for snacks or control of Spotify. Rather than shouting, I pull over, turn to them and say that we are not carrying on with this journey until they stop. I refuse to start the engine again which means not going to the party, playdate or football tournament and that is usually enough to put an end to the shenanigans.

Don't Set Punishments in Anger

Dishing out punishments in the heat of the moment is not ideal – the punishment will most likely be disproportionate to the 'crime' and therefore unfair and it's also probably unsustainable and you might be shooting yourself in the foot. I saw this hilarious (and truthful) TikTok the other day where the dad tells the misbehaving child that he's taking the tablet away for a whole week while the mum stands there incredulous because she needs the respite the tablet can provide!

Don't blow up. If there has been an incident or some behaviour that needs addressing, wait until everything has died down and you can talk about it clearly and with composure.

Saying Sorry

Everyone has a breaking point and it's inevitable, no matter how hard you try to keep a lid on it, you're going to fly off the handle occasionally. When that happens, I feel awful but I know it's important to own up to it and apologise once it's all calmed down. As parents, we all have our moments. We are human.

I say something along the lines of, 'I'm sorry, I yelled. It was because of X, Y or Z, but it was the wrong thing to do and I'm going to try not to do that in the future.' It's good for your children to see you taking responsibility for mistakes and it's also showing them that shouting is not how we talk to each other.

Final Word: It might look as if I have everything under control, but a lot of the time I feel a bit like a mummy duck, gliding across the water while frantically paddling underneath!

Whatever you're going through as a parent right now, remember everything's a phase.

And you are enough.

One Last Thing . . .

Over the last few years it's become a bit of an internet trend to talk about how hard parenting is and imply that you need copious amounts of wine to get through it. It's great that we're able to be honest about the 'warts and all' of being a mum and it's definitely one of the toughest jobs in the universe, but it's also the most fulfilling and I sometimes think the negative discourse leaves very little space to shout about how beautiful motherhood can be.

And now my kids are a bit older, it's really starting to dawn on me how quickly the time goes. Scarily quick.

So whenever I create content, my number one priority is to make it as positive as possible. That has always been my focus, whether it's YouTube, Instagram or TikTok. It's been the same with this book, which I feel so proud to have been given the opportunity to write.

Thank you for reading it. I hope it's something you can keep referring back to on your parenting journey, whatever that looks like. Receiving messages from people saying that they've learned a hack or been inspired by one of my routines which has made family life that little bit easier, makes my day. That is why I do what I do and it's the best feeling knowing that it's making a difference, however small.

It's no secret that my audience is mostly female – around 98 per cent I think! – and I do believe that something very special happens when women come together as a community. It takes a village, right? Even if some of that village is online. What we've built between us through the power of social media feels quite magical. We're all here for each other and it's hard to find words that do justice to what you guys have given me over the last few years.

You have been my cheerleaders and have gifted me back my confidence. You have made me a better mum and I know that I wouldn't be here without you. I appreciate every one of you and I love the community we have grown.

This might be the end of the book, but it's not the end of the story. I remain on a mission to find the best hacks and I'll continue to share them with you all for as long as you'll have me. I'll probably be reviewing retirement cruises and walking aids before we know it!

I want to hear all about the things you wish *you'd* known, too. If you discover a hack that is worth shouting about, let me know. My DMs are always open and I'd absolutely love to hear from you. Let's keep the conversation going. Let's keep supporting and celebrating each other and finding the joy as we muddle through motherhood together.

Love, Emily xxx